D0358523

The House of Blue Lights

Also by Joe Roberts

THREE-QUARTERS OF A FOOTPRINT

The House of Blue Lights

JOE ROBERTS

BANTAM PRESS

LONDON • NEW YORK • TORONTO • SYDNEY • AUCKLAND

TRANSWORLD PUBLISHERS LTD
61–63 Uxbridge Road, London W5 5SA

TRANSWORLD PUBLISHERS (AUSTRALIA) PTY LTD
15–25 Helles Avenue, Moorebank, NSW 2170

TRANSWORLD PUBLISHERS (NZ) LTD
3 William Pickering Drive, Albany, Auckland

Published 1995 by Bantam Press
a division of Transworld Publishers Ltd

A catalogue record for this book is available
from the British Library
ISBN 0593 035259

Typeset in 11/13pt Goudy by
Falcon Graphic Art Ltd,
Wallington, Surrey
Printed in Great Britain by
Mackays of Chatham plc, Chatham, Kent.

For my friend from Spellman's, Marion Winik,
and in her husband Tony's memory.

When a woman lives alone, her house should be extremely dilapidated, the mud wall should be falling to pieces, and if there is a pond, it should be overgrown with water-plants. It is not essential that the garden be covered with sage-brush, but weeds should be growing through the sand in patches, for this gives the place a poignantly desolate look.

From *The Pillow Book of Sei Shōnagon* (late tenth century) – translated from the Japanese by Ivan Morris.

The House of Blue Lights

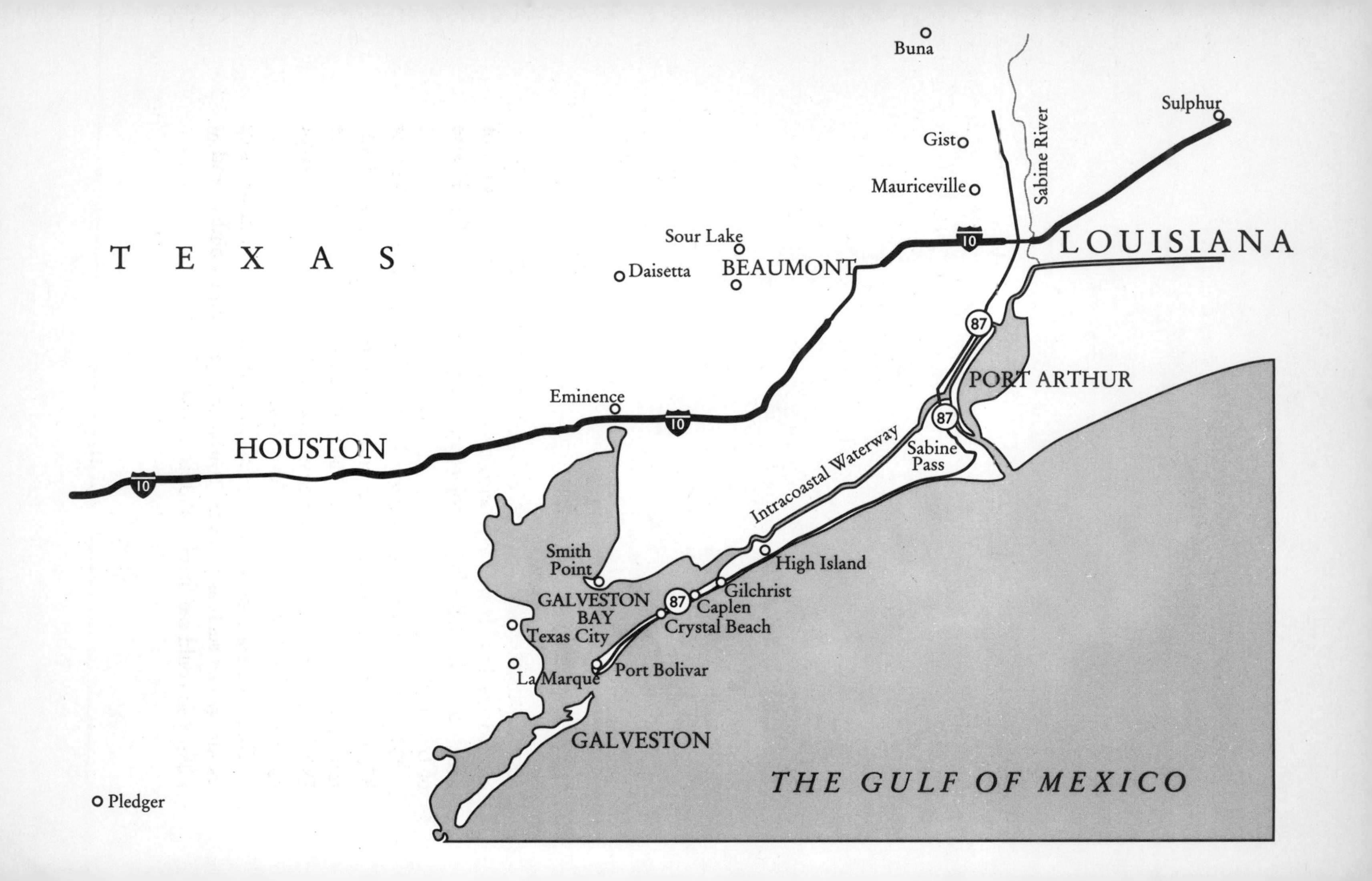
Buna
Sulphur
Gist
Sabine River
Mauriceville
Sour Lake
LOUISIANA
T E X A S
Daisetta
BEAUMONT
10
87
PORT ARTHUR
Eminence
87
HOUSTON
Sabine Pass
Intracoastal Waterway
10
Smith Point
High Island
Gilchrist
GALVESTON BAY
Caplen
Texas City
Crystal Beach
Port Bolivar
La Marque
GALVESTON
THE GULF OF MEXICO
Pledger

One

YOU COULD SEE MARY ALICE'S BEACH HOUSE FROM THE FERRY THAT crossed the bay. It was blue with an orange roof, from the eaves of which dim blue light bulbs projected, the majority dead. The House of Blue Lights.

When we reached the Bolivar landing I set off along Highway 87, past painted signs for guns and ammunition, seafood and bait, tattoos and barbecue, past the black Victorian lighthouse, past the Dutchman's property, to the first crossroads. Then I turned right along the curving road beside the marsh.

There were always birds – egrets and spoonbills, sometimes more exotic species such as pelicans, scarlet tanagers and catbirds – and at night you could see fireflies and hear frogs.

'Sugar in the morning,
Sugar in the evening.
Sugar at suppertime.'

Mary Alice came down the steps of the House of Blue Lights (a step was missing and the gap worried her in the dark) singing to Sweet William, her Italian greyhound. The house stood on stilts, purple bugle vine and Confederate jasmine twining wildly around them. Sweet William was a timorous dog and the cats that swarmed beneath the house tormented him. When Mary Alice sang, Sweet William swung his tail and trotted by her side and found a fragile self-confidence. Mary Alice cooed, 'Now y'all be a good boy for your mama,' and he crouched at the roadside.

Mary Alice waved to me and gathered the beer cans that were strewn in the long grass.

Sparling had been sleeping under the house since Ronny Sue had turned him out. Mary Alice had promised Ronny Sue not to take him in but, because she was a kind woman, she allowed Sparling to sleep under the house among the swarming cats. Sweet William, relieved, shot back up the steps to the safety of the deck and Mary Alice looked under the house to see if Sparling was about. He was so skinny he could hide among the tall malvaceous weeds (the unchecked red and yellow hibiscus) and the scattered crates and washing-machine parts if Ronny Sue wandered by. But Mary Alice found only a tight bundle of clothes that he had been using as a pillow and a polythene bag containing eggshells.

The room that I rented from Mary Alice was quite airless; none of the four windows would open, so Sparling had helped me to wrench one of the frames off – 'Skeeters gone drive you crazy,' he warned me, his voice buzzing as if driven by a chain. A low-flying aircraft sprayed the area with insecticide. 'That don't do diddly-squat against *these* skeeters.' Sparling grinned pessimistically. 'Soon as they hear that old airplane, these skeeters take cover.' I had brought Jungle Formula repellant.

There was no bed in the room. I spread two ragged sheets over a corduroy sofa. Close up, the sofa had a peculiar damp smell, as if it had been dredged from the marsh; but it was dry, without mildew.

I found a box fan, which I placed in the frameless window, and a large standard lamp with a polished stone base that belonged, I was told, to one of the attendants on the ferry. There was a dainty-looking wardrobe that was full of welding equipment. Resting against the side of the wardrobe was a portrait of Elizabeth Taylor as Cleopatra, painted on black velvet.

Because I had a door that I could close, I had some privacy. The front door was never closed: neighbours came and went whether Mary Alice was in or out.

The rest of the house, apart from a small bathroom at the far end, was open-plan. Mary Alice's bed, television and video, and two more decrepit sofas (one functioning as a clothes pile, the other as Sweet William's bed) occupied a far corner. Various cardboard boxes contained her possessions; a box of romantic novels, a box of jigsaw puzzles and a box she called her 'casket of memories', full of letters and photographs. By the front door was a telephone that would not accept outgoing calls.

Along another wall was the kitchen; Mary Alice generally ate at work, or with her friend Lucilla, so it was no longer operational. The sink was full of smeary glasses and more than a hundred empty bottles stood on the sideboard. There was no refrigerator, just a styrofoam ice-chest, usually with water and floating labels in it.

The boxes and the sparsity of household articles gave the impression that Mary Alice had recently moved to the House of Blue Lights, that more belongings were on their way and those that had arrived were not yet unpacked. In fact, Mary Alice had lived there for eleven years.

Equally, a stranger coming in might suppose that a party had taken place the night before, that a space had been cleared for dancing. It always looked like that.

There were parties of course but they were impromptu affairs; Mary Alice and a few friends sitting out on the deck or the steps when somebody would drive up with a couple of bottles of whisky or a case of beer on the back of his truck, asking, 'You gonna help me drink this or what?'

A typically laconic reply: 'Guess we *could* just 'bout destroy the evidence for you.'

Mary Alice worked as a waitress at the Homestead on the island, five minutes from the ferry landing, a restaurant that stayed open all day and all night, and this was her day off. The night before she had worked from 10 p.m. until 6 a.m., serving 'ranch-house' breakfasts to fishermen and wrapping cutlery in paper napkins for the girls on the morning shift. Then she had driven her mustard-coloured Chevrolet Impala over to the Bellizaire Apartments to visit Captain Guidry who was always up early because he had trouble sleeping. There she had stayed until half past ten.

When she left the Bellizaire Apartments Mary Alice went to Gerlands to buy food for Sweet William and some for the cats that, out of kindness, she was inclined to feed. Heading in the general direction of the ferry, she drove along Sixth Street to Blue Flame Liquor and bought a pint of peppermint schnapps.

□ □

The greater part of the Texas coastline – which curves southward from the west bank of the Sabine River, the border of Louisiana, to the north bank of the Rio Grande, the border of Mexico – consists of bays and lagoons, fed by a mixture of salt water and fresh water from various rivers, and 'barrier islands' – which in many cases are not islands at all but extended peninsulas, fingers of land. Inland from these barrier islands are the sticky marshes and wetlands that merge in turn into the featureless coastal plains. The barrier islands protect the mainland from tropical cyclones and hurricanes.

Shrimp, crabs and all kinds of fish live off these islands, so there are many boats – but fishing is not what it was. Chemical spillage and the ravages of the economy have taken their toll. Conservationists have ruled that the nets must be fitted with special valves, turtle-excluder devices, which, the shrimpers protest, drastically reduce their hauls. The repossession of boats is common.

Some shrimpers look to the oilfields for work, where, as unskilled labourers, they are given menial jobs; some have suffered dreadful injuries and exist on settlements from the insurance companies.

Now Vietnamese immigrants have entered the seafood business. They operate in a more intensive and methodical way than the original shrimpers, controlling every stage from fishing to retail, and their presence has led to some ugly altercations; the Ku Klux Klan have burnt Vietnamese boats. Many of the white shrimpers seem to be Vietnam veterans (an upbringing in steamy swampland made them peculiarly suited to the combat conditions of South East Asia) and that adds piquancy to the rivalry. In Port Bolivar I never saw any Vietnamese but in Port Arthur and all along the Louisiana coast there are large communities of these new immigrants.

Such sodden land precludes much agriculture but rice can be grown on the prairies beside the Sabine. Further south the landscape becomes more arid and the wetlands give way to scrub.

The Bolivar Peninsula (named in honour of the South American liberator by the explorer and revolutionist Henry Perry in 1815) is the first of the barrier islands; it stretches some thirty miles southwesterly, from Sabine Pass at one end to Port Bolivar at the other; then there are three miles of sea to the eastern tip of Galveston Island, the next in the chain. A ferry service operates; many people who work in the city of Galveston prefer to live on the more rural peninsula. At its broadest, between Caplen and Crystal Beach, the peninsula is three and a quarter miles; at its narrowest, the area called Rollover Pass, it measures less than a quarter of a mile. Actually a map gives the peninsula three humps like a sea serpent.

Galveston Island is another strip, narrower still than the peninsula and twenty-seven miles long, that stands at the mouth of Galveston Bay. The city of Galveston occupies much of the eastern end.

The northern shore of the Bolivar Peninsula faces both the Intracoastal Waterway (a partly natural, partly man-made, canal that runs from Florida to Mexico) and the eastern waters of Galveston Bay. The gap between Port Bolivar and Galveston Island allows ships to pass from the Gulf of Mexico into the bay, and across the bay to the Houston Ship Canal. The southern shore faces the blue and brown sea. Marine traffic along both shores, and in both directions, is constant.

Highway 87 runs the full length of the peninsula but storm damage has closed part of it since 1980. At High Island (a hill that only becomes an island in the event of a flood and is, in fact, the roof of a vast subterranean salt dome) Highway 87 is intersected by Highway 124, which crosses the waterway into Chambers County and leads to a town called Winnie. If one were to travel along the peninsula on, say, foot or horseback, most of the landscape would be marshy, the vegetation chiefly salt grasses of more botanical than aesthetic interest. Galveston Island is where the marshes metamorphose into salt meadows beyond which the dunes rise. Sea oats, dove weeds and goat weeds grow there. All along the coastline snakes abound: cottonmouths and diamond-back rattlers.

This is land that only eases itself out of the water. Lethargy hangs like a miasma and it is humid all year round. The sky is huge, sagging with tired clouds, and the marshes are choked with litter, brown bags full of cans, even half-submerged cars.

It is the custom, on sweltering evenings, to cook outdoors; dark silhouettes stand beside glowing pits and the sweet aroma of burning ketchup is carried on the heavy air.

§

In the summer of 1722 a French sea captain called Simars de Bellisle and four companions were marooned on the peninsula by a mutinous crew. The five had to fend for themselves; they had their rifles, a little ammunition and some biscuits. Bellisle was not particularly worried for he believed they were close to the mouth of the Mississippi. Trudging along the peninsula in a vaguely eastward direction, the party soon realized that Bellisle was mistaken.

Then the ammunition ran out and, one by one, the four companions fell by the wayside, starving and exhausted. Bellisle continued and was walking the eastern shore of Galveston Bay, existing on birds' eggs, grass and yellow tree worms, when he was set upon by Orcoquisa Indians.

The Orcoquisas tore off Bellisle's European clothing – they had never seen a white man before – and carried him back with them to the peninsula, where he was initially treated as an equal, accompanying the Orcoquisas in their continual search for food.

It seems that the natives of this unpromising land fared very little better than had complete aliens, and many of their habits (for example, returning to their self-induced vomit, to enjoy a meal twice) disgusted the Frenchman. The Orcoquisas, in turn, became bored with their squeamish guest and, as winter drew in, they started to treat him spitefully, beating him with green sticks and forcing him to search for firewood, and to travel on foot while they rode horses; until one day the Orcoquisas crossed paths with a band of Caddo warriors, who rescued Bellisle, carrying him across the Sabine River to the French fort at Natchitoches.

The Orcoquisas and the Caddos were not the only Indians wandering the dunes and coastal marshes; from the western edge of Galveston Bay to the vicinity of Corpus Christi stretched the dominions of the Karankawas.

They were known to the French as the *Quelancouchis*. The Lipan name for the tribe was *Nda kun-dadehe*, which means 'people walking in the water'. The Tonkawas called the tribe *Yakokon kapai* ('without moccasins'), but that was how they referred to all the coastal tribes. The name Karankawa apparently means 'fond of dogs' – which is ambiguous because, whilst otherwise treating them with consideration, Karankawas, like many Indians, ate their dogs; indeed a dog was considered just as edible as a deer or a pig.

There were five tribes: the Coapite Karankawas, the Coco Karankawas, who lived on Galveston Island and at the mouth of the Brazos River, the Karankawas of Matagorda Bay, the Kohani Karankawas at the mouth of the Colorado River, and the Copano Karankawas, for whom Copano Bay is named.

The first European to meet them was Alonso Alvarez de Piñeda, who explored the Spanish territories north of the Rio Grande. There was some disagreement, and the Karankawas killed him.

Nine years later, a shipwreck brought eighty Spanish sailors to the island. They were under the command of Alvar Nuñez Cabeza de Vaca; they had drifted, starving, across the Gulf of Mexico from Florida, after a disastrous exploratory expedition. They landed on Galveston Island in the winter of 1528.

The Karankawas called the island *Auia*, which might have been onomatopoeic, to suggest the sough of the wind and the waves. Cabeza de Vaca called the place *Malhado*, the island of misfortune.

The first encounter was friendly enough; the Karankawas gave the Spaniards food, and the Spaniards patched up their rafts and attempted to sail on down to Mexico. Less than a hundred yards offshore the rafts capsized and the sailors lost most of their belongings; a few men drowned, the rest struggled back to the strand, where the Karankawas (inclining emotionally towards pathos) cried for half an hour, then led the Spaniards to their camp where they were given more food, and shelter, and a great welcoming celebration with all-night dancing.

Malnutrition and dysentery started to kill off the Spaniards. European germs infected and killed some of the Indians. There were only sixteen sailors left, no longer such welcome guests. Cabeza de

Vaca's men were enslaved for six years, whilst the commander himself was employed as a hesitant medicine man, and as a trader between hostile tribes.

Cabeza de Vaca and three others escaped in time, walking all the way across to the Pacific coast of Mexico, to rejoin Spanish civilization. His account of the Karankawas terrified the colonists, who, for a long time afterwards, left the coastal regions north of the Rio Grande unoccupied.

Cabeza de Vaca's sixteenth-century account describes the Karankawa men as tall and well-built, wearing no clothing at all but inserting lengths of cane through holes pierced in their nipples and lower lips. The older women wore garments made of Spanish moss, the younger women wore deerskins.

The Karankawas ate prickly pears and assorted roots, spiders, worms, caterpillars, lizards, snakes and ant eggs.

Their pottery was distinctive: wide-mouthed jars, globular ollas and high-sided bowls, coated inside and decorated outside with asphalt. The pots were used for roasting and boiling.

They constructed cane weirs to trap fish. To hunt they used longbows or dug pits; occasionally herds of buffalo crossed their territory. Cabeza de Vaca's description of the buffalo is the earliest given by a European.

The Karankawas were apparently kind to their children (who, as infants, were fastened to cradle boards, which also served to flatten their foreheads) and equable amongst themselves, sharing what possessions anyone had. They built only the most ephemeral of dwellings. They were without medicine, treating illness by blowing gently and optimistically upon the sick.

An oblique humour was indulged: to get rid of the mosquitoes that plagued them, the Indians sometimes set the grass alight. That was a jokey thing to do; the very idea had them in stitches.

There is nothing to suggest the man-eating that has, for centuries, been associated with the Karankawas. Some of Cabeza de Vaca's own men practised cannibalism at the point of starvation. Perhaps it was the breaking of the taboo, not by the Karankawas themselves but within their tribal territories, that led to their reputation; the information received in disgust by neighbouring tribes such as the Tonkawas and then distorted, over the generations, before being passed back to the white man.

The Karankawas believed in a pair of divinities, *Pichini* and *Mel*, to whom they prayed for abundance in fishing and hunting and victory in battle. Their priests were called *Comas* and their religious celebrations – there were several kinds – were called *Mitotes*. A festival of thanksgiving, after a successful hunting or fishing expedition, involved the ingestion of a tea made from the leaves of the yupon shrub (*Ilex cassine*). The tea was black, with golden lights, and made frothy by pouring it from a raised platform into the drinking vessel. Only Karankawa men were allowed the drink; as soon as it was ready, the *Coma* would call the equivalent of 'Tea's up!' and the women had to stop what they were doing and stay where they were; any woman caught moving around would be beaten and, should one pass the *Coma* in the act of brewing, the tea would be thrown away, for it was believed to be contaminated by a woman's presence: the drinker would sicken and die.

The tea, strangely, had no intoxicating effects, but a *Mitote* might last as long as three days and three nights and an individual might quaff up to five gallons over such time, chanting about fish and women and the majesty of the sun.

Turtle-shell tambourines were banged, gourds filled with pebbles were rattled, and reed pipes were blown to produce an odd sepulchral quacking.

Witnesses have described the music as harsh and melancholy but hypnotic; it might have sounded like Ornette Coleman's *Dancing In Your Head* album or the *chuncho* music of the Andes.

The chanting was, on occasion, led by a young man, covered completely with animal skins, who walked on all fours. A great fire was lit on the beach and around it danced the Karankawa men with exaggerated lurching, leaping movements. The movements were not spontaneous but choreographed.

By the beginning of the nineteenth century the preferred refreshment was whisky but, even intemperate, the *Mitotes* never slackened into improvisation.

•

Cabeza de Vaca reported the terror struck into several of the coastal tribes by the Bad Thing (*Mala Cosa*).

The Bad Thing was a hirsute and demonic dwarf who came out at night to mutilate sleeping Indians. He carried a flint hatchet and a burning brand. The Bad Thing would wake his victim, dazzle him with the flame, then deeply gash his stomach with the hatchet. Having made a large hole, the Bad Thing stuck his hand in and pulled out some of his victim's entrails. These he would sever with the hatchet and throw onto the embers of the campfire. Sometimes he hacked off an arm. The most extraordinary demonic power the Bad Thing had was to be able, with a touch, to heal the wound or replace the severed arm without leaving a scar. The victim was weak and in shock for a day or two after the ordeal but otherwise unharmed. It seems strange that the rest of the tribe slept on while the dwarf was operating.

Once the Bad Thing attended a *Mitote*, as an onlooker. The Indians saw their chance to placate the fiend. He was offered yupon tea and victuals but he refused.

They asked the Bad Thing where he lived and he pointed to the nearby marsh, answering, 'That is where I live, under the black water. That marsh is the roof of my house.'

So the *Mitote* progressed, and the dancing verged on the ecstatic, and the Bad Thing joined the dance for he had learnt the steps; except he performed them faster than the others and he weaved between the dancers with rapid, precise movements.

Around and away spun the dwarf, in and out of the shadows and the flickering lights.

Suddenly he was gone and the Karankawas heard a sequence of splashes. They knew the demon had retired to his house beneath the marsh.

The Karankawas performed arcane funeral rituals. When a young man died, his family mourned for an entire year. Before dawn, at noon, and at sunset, relatives ritually wept for the deceased. When the year passed, there was a ceremony involving purification of the mourners by smoke and the young man was never mentioned again.

Old people were not mourned at all.

The Karankawa dead were buried in shallow graves near the campsites. A *Coma* was not buried but cremated during a ceremonial *Mitote*. The *Coma*'s ashes were kept and, exactly one year after the cremation, mixed into the yupon tea to be drunk by his successor and his relatives.

Popular male pastimes, besides *Mitotes*, were hatchet-throwing and archery, all-in wrestling and wife-swapping. Some Karankawa men became eunuchs; they were called *berdaches*. The *berdaches* wore women's clothing and accompanied the warriors into battle against other tribes; they did not fight but herded the stolen horses. Often a brave kept both a wife and a *berdache*. Although he might happily exchange his wife for another, a *berdache* was his alone.

The Karankawas had great reverence for a marine sunset; daily they would observe the wonderful sight as if spellbound, remaining quite silent and still, until the sun was fully set and the shore was dark around them.

Spanish missionaries tried for centuries to convert the five tribes, but in vain. Father Joseph Escovar directed a mission among the Copano Karankawas in the 1750s and 1760s. He succeeded with just twenty-one baptisms – twelve adults and nine children – all *in articulo mortis*, for the conversion of the healthy was out of the question. Escovar's mission was inspected by Father Gasper José de Solis:

> The most part of them are in the woods or on the banks of some of the many rivers, or with another nation also Karankawas, their friends and confederates on the shore of the sea . . .
>
> They are all barbarous, idle, lazy; and although they are so greedy and gluttonous that they eat meat almost raw, parboiled or half-roasted and dripping with blood, yet rather than stay in the mission where the padre provides them with everything

> needed to eat and wear, they prefer to suffer hunger, nakedness and other necessities, in order to be at liberty and idle in the woods or on the beach, giving themselves up to all kinds of vice, especially lust, theft and dancing.

The eighteenth-century Spanish missionaries insisted that the Karankawas were cannibals. Though no Spaniard ever witnessed the atrocity, they left detailed secondary accounts of anthropophagic rituals. Perhaps there was a grain of truth. Many American Indians desecrated the corpses of slain enemies; the practice of scalping falls within this tradition. There is evidence that some Indians cut off (and possibly consumed) parts of their slain enemy's bodies – a ritual act of magic and revenge far removed from the depraved feast implied by the missionaries, wherein human flesh is treated as meat to satisfy profane hunger.

The last Karankawa died on Galveston Island in 1858.

In 1891 a Dr Gatschet published two vocabularies of the Karankawa language: one obtained from the Tonkawa Indians, and the other from the recollections of Mrs Alice Williams Oliver, who had lived near one of the tribes as a girl and had written her own account: our last glimpse of the Karankawas.

> When the Indians conversed they carefully husbanded or somewhat repressed their breath and, at the end of a sentence or isolated word, it escaped in a gentle sigh or 'breathing' – giving the speakers an air of *ennui*; this was heightened by their 'conversational' expression which was stolid and slightly contemptuous, and by their custom of never looking at the person to whom they were talking, as if their speech was an act of utter condescension.

The men she recalls as tall and sturdy, with long black matted hair, sometimes decorated with a rattlesnake's rattle, but the women Mrs Oliver considered short, stout and disagreeable. Both sexes wore deerskin bracelets and simple skirts. The children generally went naked. Everyone was dirty and smelt of the shark oil that they used to repel mosquitoes. Both men and women had blue spiralling tattoos on their faces.

They migrated to the island each October, either on foot, crossing a ford called Karankawa Reef, or by rowing crudely fashioned canoes. They ate deer, fish, oysters, turtles, berries, nuts and persimmons, but were ignorant of corn and agriculture. Most of the time they got drunk and begged from the settlers, who found them a nuisance.

The Karankawas were enigmatic in their attitude to the settlers. Fear and surliness mingled with aloof fascination and resentful dependence. They were not unstintingly hostile. Mrs Oliver includes an anecdote of Karankawas bringing fresh water to the sick child of a settler.

Gradually they started to retreat, or were driven, into northern Mexico, where they were absorbed into other tribes.

Two

MARY ALICE'S CHILDHOOD WAS SPENT IN JASPER COUNTY, WHICH IS INLAND, north of Beaumont and Port Arthur. Her parents were divorced when she was four. Her father moved to Buna, and she was raised by her mother and grandmother, beauticians after a fashion, in the little town of Gist.

Shortly after the divorce both women found religion of a grim, fearful variety. Thereafter, Mary Alice's days were blighted: listening to the radio was sinful, as was reading anything other than the Bible, as was eating ice-cream.

When Mary Alice was eight, a new preacher came to the church and, after the briefest courtship, married her mother.

The preacher was considerably younger than his bride. He was a small, sickly man, with bright yellow skin and black hair that was always wet, who could not grow a beard and was given to fits. Mary Alice was taught to hold her stepfather's mouth open so that he would not bite his tongue off.

A rumour got about that the preacher was only thirteen years old, the runaway son of a café proprietor in Daisetta. This was not the case: the café proprietor drove over to Gist and agreed that the preacher was not his boy. The sheriff demanded to see the preacher's birth certificate anyway. The preacher, unable to produce such a document, insisted that he was twenty-one years old, and the matter was dropped until, six months later, a truck-driver from New Braunfels recognized the preacher as Little Nathan the Boy Canary.

Whether this was the preacher's true identity remains a mystery, for the very next day he succumbed to a fit, alone at the wheel of his car, and was found dead (the car pulled up tidily at the side of the road) just outside Mauriceville. The preacher had not bitten his tongue off but he had choked on it.

After that, Mary Alice's mother and grandmother became more severe in their righteousness, and they stopped going to church because Grandmother believed that the preacher to replace her son-in-law was spreading typhoid fever.

Mary Alice's mother took to preaching herself. Filled with the Holy Spirit, she slunk about whining and searching for money. Then she would catch the bus to Beaumont, where she tended to preach in bars.

One evening she was thrown out of the Lucky Deuce for speaking in tongues; the barman found her behaviour alarming. She was consequently arrested for disorderly conduct, an indictment that the gossips back in Gist altered to public intoxication, as that was an indictment more shaming than disorderly conduct upon a preaching woman.

When Mary Alice was eleven years old, 'just a funny little kid', she experienced incubus trouble.

At first she thought a cat had jumped through her bedroom window. The cat lay over her mouth as if to suffocate her; then it put its own mouth over hers and tried to suck the air out of her lungs. 'It was soft but it could push.' When Mary Alice broke free she saw that she was quite alone in her bedroom.

A string of similar and often painful traumas occurred over the summer, until she was scared to fall asleep; she would lie awake in the darkness, warding off the incubus with gospel songs she had learned from the Blackwood Brothers and Molly O'Day.

One night her singing woke her mother and grandmother, who demanded an explanation. When Mary Alice attempted to describe the nightmarish sensations, the women hushed her and broke into prayer.

The following night her grandmother bound Mary Alice's wrists to the bedposts. Mary Alice felt that she was being sacrificed to the incubus. She was too afraid to sing. As it turned out, there was no need, for the incubus had gone elsewhere. 'Probably to bother some other girl.'

On her twelfth birthday, Mary Alice hitch-hiked to Buna to find her father, who had become the owner of a used car lot and acquired a new wife and a stepson. The wife was a former Stonewall Peach Queen; her name was Brenda. Her son, who was also twelve, was called Repton.

Mary Alice became a 'lot puppy', a very greasy child playing in and beneath parked cars. Repton became her best friend ('He was a courteous boy, he never tried anything nasty') and Mary Alice's teens were radiantly happy, for she was the most beautiful and desired girl at her high school. A certain teenage optimism had endured in her personality.

Mary Alice's mother and grandmother, for all she knew, still lived in Gist.

Now Mary Alice was fifty years old and, although she had certainly gained some weight since her dancing days, she was still considered by many observers 'a fine-lookin' girl'; her legs were long and shapely and her hips slim. Mary Alice's face was still unlined; it was essentially the same as in the Buna High School Yearbook of 1959. Her eyes were large and brown, the shape of almonds, and very shiny. They brimmed easily. She had a small fine nose and a rosebud mouth with a trembling lower lip.

On days off she wore soft childish clothes; pastel T-shirts and terry-cloth shorts. She went without make-up and her complexion was freckled. At the Homestead she wore a thick beige foundation that aged her cruelly. Likewise her hair: left alone it was brown and feathery; for work it was curled and sprayed to an unnatural crispness.

Otherwise only double chins and a heavy trunk betrayed Mary Alice's age. Her increased size she attributed to German blood on her father's side.

Mary Alice's dancing days (that was how she always referred to them; they sounded Edwardian, like salad, or halcyon, days) had been in Dallas in the 1970s, after she had left Herm, her 'no-count' husband, also a used-car salesman, in the town of Sour Lake.

'Where's Sour Lake, Mary Alice?'

'It's along 105, between Batson and Beaumont.' Mary Alice spoke with a childish slur, as if her tongue was fractionally too thick for her mouth; this was accentuated by alcohol.

Herm was a small-town big shot who put about the image of himself as 'beaver-crazy'. He talked a lot about Hugh Hefner and the Playboy Philosophy – Herm had saved and bound every issue of the magazine since August 1961 – and he harassed his female employees (telephonists and finance clerks) so rigorously that more than one, before resigning, had spoken tearfully to Mary Alice.

When it came to marital sex, Herm found himself with a wife whose appetite was as strong as his own, and that scared him. Herm liked to badger women into submission and to feel that the sexual act degraded them; neither was the case with Mary Alice so he left her alone.

'I wanted to holler. I have a heart that runs to lovin' first, not diamonds and rubies. I had me a husband who just couldn't see it,' she confessed. After two years of marriage she took a Buick from his lot and headed up Interstate 45.

In Dallas she made the acquaintance of Billy Bob Edelman, who was a millionaire – to do, Mary Alice figured, with real estate – and who proclaimed, 'There just can't be anything more exciting than a real nice pretty girl that's thoughtful and has an air about her.' Billy Bob Edelman knew lots of other millionaires (oilmen and developers, mostly) and celebrities (politicians, footballers and country singers). He also knew many pretty girls (Braniff stewardesses, cheerleaders and dancers from the Rio Room) and his hobby was introducing the millionaires and celebrities to the pretty girls.

Billy Bob Edelman's parties were frequent, the wildest in Dallas. Usually one or more of the pretty girls would be persuaded to dance naked (or at least topless) on the little stage he had built in the long recreation room, and the day came when Mary Alice was persuaded. She made $2,400 in tips. 'Hell, I wasn't lookin' back.'

For five years Mary Alice lived in a condominium with a chandelier in the reception room, an original Gorman in the Southern Colonial snuggery and a log-edged swimming pool; a cherry-coloured BMW, holidays in Acapulco and Vail and weekends in Las Vegas. All her sugarmen were perfect gentlemen and, once or twice, marriage was proposed, but, 'Un huh, baby, I wasn't going back there.'

Mary Alice's greatest triumph was the night she danced for Elvis Presley, whom she had adored since girlhood. He came to Billy Bob Edelman's house in 1975, with his personal doctor and about ten sidekicks. 'Most of the girls fooled with the sidekicks,' said Mary Alice, 'but I just went straight up to Elvis himself and told him that I loved every single song he had ever recorded. And, I'm telling you, he was the handsomest man I ever set eyes on.'

'Wasn't he pretty fat by that time?'

'Hell, most of the fellows around were fatter than he was, Joseph baby. Money makes a man fat. Ain't nothin' wrong with fat on a gentleman like Elvis.'

'What was he wearing?'

'Oh, he looked real fetchin', all in black with a bright yellow tie and the biggest belt I've ever seen with blue diamonds sparklin' around the buckle and a gold chain with some kinda government medal on it and a pearl-handled pistol in a shoulder holster. And I recall he had real dainty feet, tiny-lookin' feet, and he was wearin' lizard ropers. He was real majestic.'

Elvis had taken her hand and said, in a low breathy voice, 'Mary Alice, honey, you just as pretty as a turtle dove. I would be mighty honoured if you'd dance for me and my personal doctor and the boys here.'

Billy Bob Edelman (circulating with a tray of barbecued pork ribs) leant over and whispered, 'Now, Elvis, you gotta make it worth the lady's while.' Elvis had nodded and replied, 'Yes, sir.'

That Elvis should call Billy Bob Edelman 'sir' seemed to Mary Alice so sweet and polite that she declared, 'Shoot, worth my while the heck! Why, it would be an honour for me to entertain Mr Presley and these here gentlemen from Tennessee,' and everybody clapped and whooped.

A week or so later, Mary Alice was sent a first-class return ticket to Las Vegas. As soon as she landed at the Hughes Air Terminal, one of the sidekicks, whose name was Bubba Wing, was there to take her up to the Imperial Suite at the International Hotel where, although it was five in the afternoon, Elvis was still asleep.

Mary Alice sat at his bedside (it was like visiting a hospital) and noticed that there was aluminium foil spread over all the windows. Bubba Wing announced, 'We can wake him in about a half-hour,' and telephoned the kitchen to order some breakfast. Then Mary Alice saw the personal doctor arrive, heading straight for the bathroom, and after that three servants wheeled in a trolley of breakfast food: grits, biscuits, crisp bacon, scrambled eggs, pork chops, white gravy, pickled okra, a bowl of red apples and a bowl of white cherries.

'Just step outside a moment, would ya, honey?' Bubba Wing asked Mary Alice.

When she came back in, Elvis was up, dressed in a burgundy velour tracksuit, tucking into a good Southern breakfast, and he was pleased to see her, his 'little turtle dove flown from Dallas'.

The person who most enjoyed Mary Alice's Elvis story was Lucilla.

She was younger than Mary Alice (but not as preserved – big-boned to begin with, she had become somewhat stout), and a widow whose husband, Charlie, a shrimper, had died of liver cirrhosis.

Lucilla, whose trailer (beside a struggling pecan tree) was a short walk from the House of Blue Lights, sought solace not, as was the local custom, in the bottle but in cooking and tie-dying.

She would arrive with two plates of food – it might be fried chicken livers, glazed carrots and corn pudding – and she would be wearing the most dazzling psychedelic T-shirt. Mary Alice would say with great sincerity, 'My, Lucilla, you are a burst of colour today; y'all look just like a hillside of wild flowers,' and Lucilla would reply that tie-dying was inexpensive and simple.

They would eat sitting out on the wooden steps, and afterwards when Sweet William was licking the plates, which didn't bother either of them, Lucilla would produce a very thin reefer from the breast pocket of her T-shirt, offering some to Mary Alice who always declined. 'That damn stuff just muzzes me and, baby, I'm dizzy enough.'

So Lucilla smoked her reefer alone and pressed Mary Alice for more details about Elvis Presley because she too had loved him since girlhood. Mary Alice sipped at the schnapps that smelt like mouthwash – that was part of its appeal: 'There is nothing less becomin' to a real nice pretty girl than liquor breath and that's a fact' – and she would recall that when Elvis sang 'What Now, My Love?' he was looking her straight in the eye; it was the single most romantic moment of her entire life. If Lucilla, emboldened by the marijuana, urged, 'But, yeah, yeah, what was he like in bed?' Mary Alice, depending on how far down the pint of schnapps she was, would either reply, 'I would only cheapen the whole experience by discussin' it,' or she would admit: 'He was just so tired, he lay snorin' in my arms like a puppy dog.' Both answers were equally satisfying to Lucilla.

But Mary Alice would have to be very drunk to tell Lucilla about the rude man called James who had burst in a few hours later and shaken her awake, saying, 'We gotta get ya outta here, girl,' and how Elvis had just continued sleeping in a most ungentlemanly way, and how, outside the bedroom door, Bubba Wing had bad-temperedly peeled $5,000 from his wallet, with the warning, 'Now y'all don't tell a damn soul about this, ya hear.' Mary Alice was never sure what was to be kept secret: that she had been invited into Elvis Presley's bed or that so very little had taken place.

□ □

I had not been to Galveston for ten years.

I left America, where I had lived for seven years, in 1984. I was married to a girl called Nadia Williams and we lived in Austin. Nadia was from La Marque, which is on the mainland, just across the bridge on Interstate 45, beyond Tiki Island and Bayou Vista. When we visited Nadia's mother, Misia, herself the child of Russian *émigrés*, brought up in Geneva and London, we would borrow her rusty Belvedere and drive to the island.

The character of the place was ramshackle: broken things were left unmended; the hulk of a school bus (no wheels or engine) abandoned on the beach; derelict buildings with their doors creaking and sighing; the blackened timbers of a cabin. It was often hazy.

(Quite by coincidence Mary Alice had bought the Belvedere from Misia for $200 in 1984. I mentioned the car to her and she told me, 'I had one of them for a while. I bought it off a big old Polish lady. I think she lived over by Texas City. She was real strange, she cut her own hair and wore overalls.'

That sounded like Misia.

'I seen her in Galveston a couple of times afterwards, gettin' ice-cream at the drugstore. Told me she could only eat ice-cream because she had difficulty swallowin'. She used to eat triple scoops. I heard she died. That Belvedere sure did.'

'Mary Alice, that was my mother-in-law.'

'Well, shoot! It's a small world now, ain't it?')

Next to La Marque is Texas City, a conglomeration of oil refineries and chemical plants, that sprawls some way down the western shore of Galveston Bay. At night it glows, like a city in the ancient world lit by fire.

As soon as the Belvedere crossed the bridge, I felt that we had left solid ground. Galveston has a marked insularity, there is even the sensation that it is a floating island, but it is really a substantial place with 65,000 residents. The Bolivar Peninsula, by comparison, is far less populated, its 4,000 residents dispersed across five communities: in order of size, the incorporated city of Crystal Beach, Port Bolivar, Gilchrist, High Island and Caplen.

□ □

In Galveston, above Porretto Beach, there is a motel built to resemble a small ocean liner; it even has a funnel on its roof.

Around the motel are shops selling towels and T-shirts and seashells, and such baroque curios as dried sea-horses and comic figures modelled from coral. You can rent polystyrene boogie-boards, two-seater tricycles (with fringed canopies) and roller-skates.

One shop is run by an Algerian who wears a kepi; he has invented a kind of lemon sorbet called Frostball and is on the lookout for investors. Once I tried a Frostball: it tasted mainly of ascorbic acid and stained my mouth a deep indelible saffron.

All through the week these businesses seem desolate, surrounded by empty premises and boarded windows. The sun beats down and a soporific breeze comes in from the sea; there is little if any custom.

Very near the motel there is a large teaching hospital, the University of Texas Medical Branch, surrounded by cranes. Helicopter-ambulances land on one of its roofs. All over Galveston there are doctors and specialists and many senior citizens. The hospital has a burns unit; I often saw burnt people on the beach, some more like gaunt featherless birds than human beings. There is a chemical dependency unit as well; many of the patients return to the community with employment on the island, near the hospital. This part of America is full of alcoholics.

At weekends Galveston is crowded; it is the nearest seaside resort to Houston, the great metropolis some fifty miles inland. Teenagers flock down Interstate 45 in pick-up trucks and Volkswagen buses to the beaches (East Beach, Porretto Beach, Stewart Beach and West Beach) that become dirty and noisy.

The teenagers tend to dress and talk like surfers but few practise the sport, for the waves are, for the most part, sheepish. So they stand around their buses and pick-up trucks talking, or they lie on the sand, and at night they build fires.

One summer's day in 1966, unexpectedly, police armed with tear gas and nightsticks descended to clear East Beach of 3,500 teenagers. A riot ensued; bottles were thrown. The cause of the police offensive was a string of complaints from visiting families, about profane language.

There are also suburban types (in their late thirties) who imagine they are in Jamaica and whose car stereos play Jimmy Cliff and Burning Spear tapes that are nearly twenty years old. White Americans still hear reggae as beach music; Bob Marley might as well have been Hawaiian. At weekends their station-wagons cruise Seawall Boulevard until late at night; there is sometimes no escaping the soundtrack of *The Harder They Come*.

In May it is very hot; figures coming towards you wobble like mirages. Seawall Boulevard smells of gas and oil and burnt rubber. There are poisonous oleanders everywhere and palm trees and intricate wooden houses coated with blistered paint.

The sea gives off a blinding glare and, most noticeably on the island, emits a low intermittent moan. The sound, which can be deafening, is caused by the uneven slope of the sea bed; some people find the sound unpleasant, disturbing. The sea has a distrusted character all along this coast, and a reputation for grotesque gestures.

Sometimes in August and September the water turns blood-red: an effect caused by a surfeit of blue-green algae, reflecting the sunshine. In 1909 there was such an influx of glowing phosphorescent fish that it was possible to read a book on the beach at two in the morning.

Portuguese men-of-war and evil-smelling seaweed (*sargassum*) can make the beaches undesirable. Blobs of sea-pitch the size of baseballs melt on the sand. The dunes are infested with ghost crabs and katydids and earwigs and an angry, resistant strain of mosquito.

§

The first European settlers of any permanence in the area were pirates, led westward from the Mississippi Delta by their chief, Jean Lafitte, who made a camp on Galveston Island.

For a man who drifts in and out of the history of Texas and Louisiana, and who was for a time a national hero, Jean Lafitte is a remarkably elusive character. Even the spelling of his surname varies: in Galveston it is Laffite, in New Orleans Lafitte – I have opted for the latter, New Orleans having the Gallic edge.

We know he had small hands and feet (*les attachés fines*), an upright, balanced posture and a bland and dignified manner. A contemporary engraving reveals a handsome, heavy-faced man with wavy hair and a drooping moustache; the hands, protruding from frilled cuffs, are indeed tiny – otherwise he resembles both General Custer and Théophile Gautier.

Lafitte spoke English correctly, while retaining a strong French accent. His left eye tended to close when he spoke, which gave some the wrong impression; his vision was perfect in both eyes.

Jean Lafitte once shot a man called Grambo, through the heart, for calling him a pirate. Lafitte insisted that he was, by profession, a privateer. There was at the time a code of respect that included privateering with such activities as filibustering; that granted an air of political radicalism above the motive of profit alone.

He was born in Bayonne on the western edge of the Pyrenees in 1780. His early life assumes a legendary vagueness: some say that he was related to the Bourbons, others that he was a close friend of Napoleon. A series of buccaneering exploits in the Bay of Bengal are attributed to Lafitte – East Indiamen ransacked, and a fortune amassed in ivory, gold dust and palm oil – but they are improbable, according to historians who refute Lafitte's navigational skills. His career was based, after all, on receiving and distributing plunder brought to his island stronghold; he rarely ventured aboard ship and, when he did so, kept well within coastal waters. There are unkind suggestions of habitual seasickness.

Jean Lafitte and his brother Pierre arrived in New Orleans in 1809, elegant men who chose an unusual livelihood: they took over a blacksmith's forge on Saint Philip, between Bourbon and Dauphine.

At night they frequented the waterfront, mixing with slavers, smugglers, all the rough traffic. The forge became an outlet for stolen goods and contraband. The Frenchmen, with their polished manners, attracted the custom of respectable merchants, planters, society figures. Silks, cut glass, champagne and brandy, gunpowder, firearms, even sides of beef, were available.

The business flourished; in time the Lafittes held the monopoly. Pierre, the cautious younger brother and the more desirous of social position, managed the New Orleans end; he cultivated politicians and civic leaders, bribed the judges and held off any legal interference.

Jean Lafitte set up headquarters on Grand Isle in the Bay of Barataria, just west of the Mississippi Delta, sixty miles from the Crescent City across the Bayou Lafourche. There he commanded a ragged navy, employing over a thousand men: drifters, fugitives; deserters from the British, American and French fleets; Irishmen, Creek Indians, Spaniards; black men from Cuba, Santo Domingo and the Slave Coast of West Africa.

All kinds of merchandise – precious metals, jewels, grain, timber, textiles, furniture, musical instruments, marble statues, clocks, the occasional slave shipment – were brought to Grand Isle. Lafitte's employees were paid generously, receiving a percentage of the sale price as commission. Orders were despatched, back across the bayou, to New Orleans.

Lafitte was fascinated by clockwork. Mechanical novelties of all kinds, from the simplest musical boxes to artificial songbirds, found their way into his collection. His most cherished automaton was a dancing doll from Spain, almost lifesize, that pirouetted on tiny wheels hidden beneath a floor-length skirt. Around the doll's neck Lafitte hung a necklace of black pearls.

•

A succession of uprisings and revolutions in Central America, the crumbling of the Spanish Empire, produced ideal conditions for piracy. The Napoleonic Wars largely occupied both the French and British navies. The American navy at the time was a fledgling service. Furthermore, although Louisiana had been sold to the United States in 1803, the people of the state were by no means patriotic – a great deal of resentment was harboured against Washington. The Government found Louisiana a notoriously difficult place.

The French-speaking populace would have had more sympathy for their compatriots, *les frères* Lafitte, than any imported Yankee legislator.

Various attempts were made by the Government to curtail their operations. Officials were sent southwards to end the racket but always returned unsuccessful; some returned full of praise for the generous Frenchmen; one district attorney, by name of Grymes, was presented with a chestful of gold coins; its value, $40,000.

By 1814 America was at war with Britain. Lafitte's enclave at the mouth of the Mississippi, and its vulnerability to the British, was causing the Government some concern.

Soon enough British envoys did sail to the island with a message for the privateer. They were invited to dine at Lafitte's mansion. Splendid delicacies – beef from Scotland and Spanish quinces – were served, fine wine flowed. Cuban musicians played fast, complicated melodies. After dinner the Spanish doll danced for the British officers.

It was put to Lafitte that he might join the Royal Navy against the Americans, with a captaincy and a sizeable fortune to be included as an incentive. Should Lafitte refuse this offer, the British swore to destroy the camp at Grand Isle. Lafitte discussed alternative strategies with his guests but they were not agreeable.

That night he sent a message to the American authorities, declaring his allegiance and asking them to come to his aid. The American navy responded by sending a large force down to Grand Isle.

They attacked and dismantled the privateer's stronghold. Lafitte and his men, in dismay, gathered what they could and fled to the bayous. The American navy now held Grand Isle and the Government had rid itself, so it thought, of the nuisance Lafitte.

General Andrew Jackson had arrived in New Orleans. Word that 12,000 British troops were marching towards the city alarmed the general, and he urgently recruited everyone available, even emptying the jails to swell the ranks. Ever the opportunist, Lafitte offered the assistance of his navy.

Such was the courage of Lafitte's navy in the Battle of New Orleans that the privateer and his men were rewarded with a full pardon by President Madison. Lafitte, basking in his new glory, asked to be reimbursed for the property ransacked by the American navy; his desire was to continue his activities on Grand Isle. Madison's amnesty did not extend that far so Lafitte cast about for a new base.

In 1816 he found a suitable alternative. Four hundred miles west of New Orleans lay the island of Galveston, more or less uninhabited.

A Frenchman, Bénard de la Harpe, had landed there in 1721 and attempted to establish a fort; the Karankawas soon drove him off but Harpe managed to draw a map of the island, which he left nameless, except for the bay which he called Port François.

In 1785 José de Evia charted the Texas coast under the command of Bernardo de Galvez, the viceroy of Mexico and formerly the Spanish governor of Louisiana. Evia's map named the island 'Isla de San Luis' and marked the eastern tip 'Pt. de Culebras' – Cobra Point. The bay to the north he labelled 'Galvestown'.

An 1804 map drawn up by Alexander von Humboldt calls the bay 'Bahia de Galveston'.

Another European had come to the island just before Lafitte, intending to make it his base. Louis-Michel Aury, a French adventurer, had joined a group of American radicals plotting to take Mexico away from Spain. Aury was also a privateer but it seems that, unlike Lafitte, politics genuinely influenced his activities. Aury formed a small band who proclaimed Galveston Island a port of the new

Republic of Mexico.

Aury's band was joined by a small fleet from Spain commanded by Francisco Xavier Mina. Mina had fled Spain after failing to overthrow Ferdinand VII. Now he saw revolutionary opportunities in the New World. Mina had toured the United States, whipping up rebellious instincts.

Soon the Frenchman and the Spaniard were joined by a small American force led by Henry Perry (who had recently named the Bolivar Peninsula) and the three of them planned their strategy.

They were an impulsive trio, fearless but not very bright, and they could not agree where to start the war. Perry wanted to attack Texas and wrest it from the Spanish, thus establishing a northern front. Mina wanted to go straight into the heart of Mexico. Aury would go wherever the action was.

The campaign was inevitably unsuccessful. Just as Lafitte was landing at Galveston, Mina was captured and shot in Mexico City.

Perry was surrounded by Spanish troops at the Presidio la Bahia and killed himself to avoid capture.

Aury, who had been prowling the Mexican coast, returned to the island to find Lafitte building a camp. Aury urged his compatriot to join him but Lafitte was dismissive, more interested in running a business than a revolution. Most of Aury's men, realizing that Lafitte was a more pragmatic chief, transferred to his navy.

Aury, disgruntled by Lafitte's attitude, sailed off to Nicaragua in search of excitement.

Lafitte, whose navy again numbered almost a thousand men and women, called Galveston Snake Island, and founded a settlement called Little Campeachy. He built himself a sturdy two-storey house surrounded by a moat, defended by four cannons; the house was painted scarlet and named La Maison Rouge.

Spain was in no position to dislodge the privateers and reluctant to turn to America for help.

Lafitte exacerbated the political situation by presenting himself as an ally to both the Spanish and Mexican forces. He even welcomed an invading French force of 150 men led by Charles Lallemand, who saw

Texas as a potential military colony that might assist Joseph Bonaparte to become King of Mexico. The quixotic brigade arrived at Galveston in January 1818. From Galveston boats went up the Trinity River to form the colony Champ d'Asile on the mainland. The Spanish soon drove the Frenchmen back to Galveston, where most of Lallemand's men, like Aury's before them, joined Lafitte's navy.

Lafitte continued his old practices: he took jewellery and textiles from captured vessels, which booty he sent overland by pack mule to his customers in New Orleans; sometimes he used the captured ships to transport their own goods to his brother; he even started selling the emptied ships back to their owners.

Slaves were sold from the island, either directly to planters who made the journey to take advantage of the large discount – slaves were sold by weight, at a dollar a pound – or to unscrupulous brokers, who marched their purchases along the Bolivar Peninsula, across country to New Orleans, and straight to the customs office, where, because the unlicensed slave trade was illegal, the broker received half the standard market value of the slaves as a reward for turning them in. The slaves were then sold on by the United States Marshal, and bought back by the brokers, who could sell their legally acquired slaves for the highest prices. The most notorious of these speculators were a pair of brothers, Resin and Jim Bowie, the latter the inventor of the eponymous knife and a hero of the Alamo.

The operation was prosperous and tightly organized, with every member of Lafitte's navy formally swearing allegiance to their commander and receiving a monthly dividend. Lafitte was a strict master, quick to hang wrongdoers, but in 1817 each of the sailors received $159 a month.

In 1818 a 62-foot sperm whale came thrashing ashore, killing a number of sailors with the swipes of its tail. The whale portended worse disasters: winds were gathering . . . The Karankawas, who were respectful of Lafitte, warned him of hurricanes.

Lafitte sheltered all the women and children inside La Maison Rouge; with his men, he sought refuge in the biggest ship, the

Saragosa.

The *Saragosa* swayed and rocked but no-one was hurt.

The storm devastated Little Campeachy, flattening La Maison Rouge, and killing those inside. Lafitte's collection was mostly destroyed. When he found the pearl necklace, then the smashed china face of the Spanish doll, he wept hysterically. Morale suffered: the men felt that Lafitte, in the selectivity of his grief, had insulted their wives and children.

A malaise overtook the operation. Dividends thereafter were lower; raids became rasher and less profitable.

The American navy grew irritated at the piracy in the Gulf, and in 1821 Lieutenant Kearney, aboard the USS *Enterprize*, sailed to Galveston and ordered Lafitte to leave the island in ninety days.

To the lieutenant's surprise, Lafitte agreed. And disappeared.

Kearney, making sure that the pirates had gone, discovered only the charred remains of a settlement.

What became of Jean Lafitte is uncertain. One story is that he sailed down to Mexico, where he continued his career, unsuccessfully, from the island of Mugeres off the Yucatan Coast; in time quitting and crossing to the mainland, where he died, penniless and drunk, in the village of Teljas. Another story has it that the great privateer adopted the name John Lafflin and moved to Alton, Illinois, where he farmed a smallholding and dealt in gunpowder until his death in 1854.

Wherever Lafitte went there followed, in his wake, tales of buried treasure. None was ever discovered at Grand Isle, and across Louisiana and coastal Texas there are sites where the hopeful, on the very best authority, have traipsed behind metal detectors and dug in vain.

On Galveston Island, Lafitte is supposed to have announced, during his final unhappy days there, that his treasure was buried beneath a copse of three trees.

The information was passed on to Walter Sherron, a chemist from Boston, who arrived in the city in 1874 only to discover that the rumour was well-known and had always proved barren. Undaunted, Sherron located the copse and set about digging a hole 400 yards east of the trees. His spade struck a solid object. The object was a large wooden casket, just smaller than the average coffin. Sherron prised the casket open and found neither doubloons nor precious stones but hundreds of keys, springs, wheels and little brass cogs.

□ □

Mary Alice told me, 'Y'all should talk to old Sparling about his treasure hunt.'

It turned out to have been a disappointing affair.

In 1985 Sparling and Ronny Sue were visiting some friends in New Orleans. The Crescent City is a mecca for heavy drinkers and both of them had plenty of money and every intention of spending it. As out-of-towners they gravitated towards the French Quarter, Bourbon Street in particular.

One morning, at half past two, they fell into conversation with an old black man called Denis Talleyrand. Talleyrand had lived in New Orleans all his life. He knew many stories that were pleasing to tourists, who in return treated him as a local 'character' and bought him plenty of drinks.

When he found out that Sparling and Ronny Sue came from the Galveston area, Talleyrand told them that Jean Lafitte's ghost had approached him once on the corner of St Philip and Decatur. Neither Sparling nor Ronny Sue believed him.

Talleyrand insisted that he had encountered the ghost shortly after midnight on 14 January 1982. Lafitte's ghost informed Talleyrand that he was descended from one of his employees, who had been wrongfully executed. He wanted to compensate Talleyrand for the death of his ancestor.

The ghost led Talleyrand to the other side of the French Market and pointed to a loose brick in the banquette. He told Talleyrand to lift the brick. Underneath there was a diamond the size of a cough drop.

Sparling and Ronny Sue were incredulous until Talleyrand took a handkerchief from his pocket and unwrapped the stone for them to inspect.

Sparling asked what happened to the ghost.

Talleyrand replied, 'He just disappeared, but 'fore he go, he says to me, "Denis, you ever needs me I'm gonna tell you how to call me, only you gotta promise to keep it secret," and I will only call Mr Lafitte down if it is absolutely necessary to do so.'

Sparling and Ronny Sue returned to the peninsula. Eighteen months later a Bolivar woman called Trudi Buford told Ronny Sue that her Great-Uncle Simpton always insisted there was buried treasure on the banks of Lake Surprise, just inland from Smith Point, on the mainland across East Bay.

A few days after that Sparling was back in New Orleans, looking for the old man on Bourbon Street.

At last Sparling found Talleyrand, who was reluctant to leave New Orleans, never having been to Texas before. Sparling entreated Talleyrand to accompany him to Bolivar, promising him one third of the bounty.

Denis Talleyrand was finally persuaded, but he warned Sparling that to seek treasure with supernatural assistance 'gonna take preparation'.

Ronny Sue had made a bed for Talleyrand in their trailer.

The old man was a most demanding guest. He would eat only if he had supervised the preparation of the food himself; that excluded any tinned or frozen food. He demanded whisky but would only drink Scotch and it had to be Johnny Walker Black Label.

Neither of his hosts was allowed to smoke around him because, even though he smoked himself, Lafitte's ghost would be confused by foreign vapours. Furthermore, Talleyrand proclaimed that Sparling and Ronny Sue should abstain from sexual relations for an entire week before the quest.

On the night of the quest Denis Talleyrand produced a bottle of scented oil; he told Sparling and Ronny Sue that this was Special Delivery Oil, with which he was to anoint them. Then he took a crowbar from his suitcase. 'When we finds the treasure this rod gonna bend.'

The three set off in Sparling's old truck and parked on Rural Route 562. For hours they wandered round and round the lake, through the tall saw-grass, in the moonlight. Ronny Sue asked Talleyrand why he didn't just summon Lafitte. 'I have done but we gotta wait.'

At half past eleven Talleyrand gave a triumphant shout. 'You see that rod bend? We found it.'

Neither Sparling nor Ronny Sue could honestly see any change in the rod but Sparling started to dig anyway. The ground was very wet and digging was difficult.

At last he found something, a small wooden box with a sturdy padlock. It was not very heavy but there was something inside it. Talleyrand, instead of sharing their excitement, was apprehensive. 'That the only box down there, you sure?'

Sparling dug deeper but found nothing else. Talleyrand assured them that the contents of the box were worthless. Ronny Sue and Sparling insisted that they open it and find out. 'I'm tellin' you,' repeated the old man, 'it got no value.'

Sparling took Talleyrand's crowbar and broke the lock. Inside the box was a leather collar and leash and an earthenware bowl with *Victor* painted on the side.

'Victor was a dog,' explained Talleyrand.

Sparling thought that was fairly obvious.

'Jean Lafitte's dog?' asked Ronny Sue, hopefully.

'No,' stated Denis Talleyrand after some consideration, 'I'd say that was my ancestor's dog.' He returned to New Orleans by bus the next day.

□ □

Between the House of Blue Lights and the marsh stood a derelict trailer, covered by creepers, thin green arms pulling it into the ground. Freakish Canna lilies, flaming azaleas and feral roses screamed in a wild plot.

I assumed the trailer was unoccupied. I mentioned it one day to Mary Alice.

'Honey, I sure wish it was empty!'

'Well, I've never seen anyone in it.'

'You never seen that old face smushed against the window?'

'No, never.'

'You never seen Miss Kinsolver?'

Miss Kinsolver was, I gathered, a recluse. She had worked for a haulage company in Houston before a long illness forced her retirement. Why she had chosen to live in Bolivar was a mystery to Mary Alice.

'She don't have nothin' to do with nobody. Darlin', she is on her own island. Fantasy Island. Oh baby, I know that's her constitutional right,' Mary Alice declared, adding rhetorically the questions: 'Am I a rock? Am I an island?' Then, seeing that I did not follow her line of thought, Mary Alice frowned. 'I know how it goes, uh huh. So long as she leaves my animals alone.'

Mary Alice told me that her neighbour detested the cats. 'Let me ask you, how could anybody hate them? I want to know, why? What is there to feel hostile about? It's a resentment that should be brought into the open.'

Miss Kinsolver had recently laid poisoned meat out for the cats. Lucilla had discovered an empty medicine container on the plank next to the china salad bowl. 'She was feeding Stelazine tablets to those kitties.'

'What is Stelazine?'

'Why, it's trifluoperazine hydrochloride, Joseph!' exclaimed Mary Alice, who could surprise me sometimes. Lucilla, I later discovered, owned a *Physician's Desk Reference* – a book to be found in a number of American households. 'Y'all mean to tell me you never heard of Stelazine?'

Had any of the cats died?

'Well, baby, it's kinda hard to tell. There are racoons just in back there; they would drag the bodies away.'

It was difficult to say how many cats there were, I would have guessed at least fifty. Some of the kittens had extra toes on their front paws. The ammoniacal smell sometimes rose up through the floor but it was just one of many smells: spilt beer, the menthol of

Sparling's cigarettes, the smell of barbecue and the mysterious damp odour of the sofa I slept on. Once or twice, the squawl of a catfight (and Sparling shouting) woke me in the night.

A few days after our conversation I did see a face at one of the windows.

Miss Kinsolver was so pale that her skin and hair were exactly the same shade, giving the impression that the face was a grey cloth that had frayed along the top, for the hair was short and ragged. She was not an old woman, perhaps forty or forty-five, and she was wearing a pale-blue nightgown that was blotched by a long brown stain. Miss Kinsolver looked worried, frightened even. Her eyes were a greyish yellow, like dish-water.

When she noticed me, she slid back from the window.

I wondered how the poor creature lived, how she looked after herself. The colourless woman, trapped in a savage garden.

□ □

Sparling was drinking Busch beer in the coffee lounge at Pirate's Cove, a motel and convenience store, run by a Gujerati consortium that had inherited the practice of extending credit to shrimpers. By his own definition Sparling was a shrimper – that is, the last job of any description that Sparling had held was aboard a shrimp boat, and that was three years ago – so he qualified. Whenever Sparling felt like getting drunk, which was often, he set out along Loop 108, the curved road beside the marsh, for Pirate's Cove.

The business, located on Highway 87 a mile from the Galveston ferry, was otherwise profitable. The Gujeratis sold bags of ice and fireworks and sun-tan lotion and gimmy-caps and cold beer and pornographic magazines and a range of processed foodstuffs that could live on the dusty shelves for years. As for fresh foods: they ran a scruffy little deli, where, beneath a catering lamp and beside a tray of enigmatically labelled 'Cajun-style' potato salad and one of fluorescent pickles, there was a hot plate, on which pieces of meat bobbed in a thick crimson gravy. Sometimes called barbecue and sometimes, if there were beans identifiable in the composition, chilli, this vivid substance – according to Lucilla, who had once proposed to run the deli counter herself, with the intention of providing 'plain wholesome food for folks new to livin' alone' – arrived, once a week, in an unmarked bucket and was to be avoided.

Sparling ate very little as a rule; Ronny Sue would cook when so inclined, which wasn't often; neither had much interest in eating.

Ronny Sue was a native of Port Bolivar. Sparling had moved there from Pledger, in Brazoria County, in the mid-1970s – 'Durin' the Ford administration,' he would state solemnly, as if the presidency had directly influenced his relocation – and they had lived together ever since Ronny Sue's husband, Mark Antony Cromie, had been sent to Huntsville for murder.

Mark Antony Cromie, at first deceived, then enraged, had stabbed to death the transvestite Stormy Monday (whose real name was Edmond Leboeuf Broussard) outside the Bengal Tiger Lounge in Port Arthur. He had served twelve years and, upon his release, disappeared to start a new life – in Washington State, Ronny Sue suspected – though for a couple of months Mark Antony Cromie was known to have worked as security consultant to a night-club in the Montrose district of Houston. During those months he hadn't once travelled down to the coast, but Ronny Sue had 'moved on' by then anyway.

Sparling was lazy and shiftless but Ronny Sue found him more biddable than Mark Antony Cromie, and she could beat him in a fight, which was agreeable because they often fought, especially when they were drunk. Afterwards Ronny Sue would take great pleasure in nursing Sparling, rubbing liniment into the bruises she had given him and sticking plasters over the skin she had broken.

It was Mary Alice's opinion that Ronny Sue's temper was due to her being 'plain-lookin' and barren with it'. Lucilla thought that it was Ronny Sue's 'bad blood, Coushatta and Irish, that's a terrible mixture' and furthermore Sparling's maternal grandfather was a full-blooded Black Seminole from Brackettville – 'So fightin's all of that Indian heritage and you gotta respect it.'

Busch was the bestselling beer at Pirate's Cove, very possibly because it was the cheapest of those with any fortitude.

Sparling was sitting on a black naugahyde sofa – which had along its backpiece a long slash that exposed its yellow foam interior – with his feet on a low table, alongside a twelve-pack of Busch and a packet of Newport Menthols.

He was watching a television programme about a woman in upstate New York who weighed more than 600 pounds; she could no longer stand up and a nurse came every day to help her wash. The enormous woman spoke with a high, piping voice. She had grown so large because she lacked self-esteem and responsive parents. 'I come from a real dysfunctional home background,' she shrieked at her interviewer, a bronzed man with unsteady bouffant hair. At the word 'dysfunctional' the interviewer started to cry. Soon the enormous woman was crying as well. 'I hear you,' the interviewer assured her, 'I hear you so well.' He turned to the camera and, wiping the tears away with a bronzed hand, pleaded: 'Do *not* go away. Please. We're gonna be here a while.' Then there were some advertisements.

Sparling offered me a beer. 'Hell, just help yourself, bub.' That surprised me because he was famously stingy.

I asked if he was comfortable sleeping under the House of Blue Lights. He looked as if he was considering the question.

'Hoo whee, six hundred pounds! Dang! I reckon that's 'bout how much a small car'd weigh!'

Sparling made springy movements, exaggerated gestures always, like an animated-cartoon character, and his thinness accentuated the impression. So, too, did his mirror-shades and his *Frosty Seafoods* gimmy-cap, which were almost shorthand for a face, in the manner of Beetle Bailey. However, if one looked closely at Sparling's features, if he kept still long enough to allow such observation, they showed themselves to be most unusual; they hinted at Tahitian or Maori ancestry.

As Lucilla had mentioned, Sparling was one quarter Black Seminole. The Black Seminoles date from the early nineteenth century. The Seminoles (who were less a tribe than a miscellany of runaway Creeks, Biloxis and Red Sticks and even a few European vagrants – the name came from *simanole*, the Creek word for 'wanderer') had fled to Florida from Mississippi in the eighteenth century.

Florida was also the destination of slaves escaping from Georgia and South Carolina. In 1819 the United States annexed Florida and the Seminoles resisted; they welcomed the escaping slaves and together the blacks and Indians withstood the white man. The Seminoles called the blacks their 'slaves' so that they could stay with them in Florida, but the blacks lived in independent settlements. The two groups often intermarried.

In the 1830s hostility between the Seminoles and the United States worsened and led to the seven-year Seminole War (1835–42). The blacks and the Seminoles fought fiercely, resisting recapture and removal, but were defeated.

The official government policy was to send Indians west into what was then called Indian Territory (it is now Oklahoma) and the Seminoles begged the Government to allow their 'slaves' to go with them. Both groups travelled west and, on the way, many of the blacks were kidnapped by slave-catchers; those that survived became more absorbed into the tribe so that, within a generation, they had merged into one race.

The Black Seminoles, as they came to be known, did not get on with other tribes in the territory and they kept escaping. They fled across Texas into northern Mexico, where they were employed by the Mexican government to keep the Apaches and Comanches at bay. They proved fearless Indian fighters and were rewarded with land at Naciamente, south of Piedras Negras.

After the Civil War, the US army approached the tribe to help rid the Fort Clark area of Comanches. The Seminole-Negro Indian Scouts were an official division from 1871 to 1914, earning several medals for bravery. There is a military cemetery at Brackettville, near Del Rio, and a small community of Black Seminoles exists there still. The last scout was buried in the cemetery in the 1950s, a man called Curly Jefferson.

When a pregnant girl called Princess came into the coffee lounge, Sparling sprang to his feet and into the shape of a question mark – he displayed an old-fashioned courtesy towards women, often addressing Mary Alice as 'Ma'am'. 'Holy shit, Princess girl, when we gone be able to dandle that sucker?'

Princess, a strong-jawed, red-haired fifteen-year-old, was clearly in the final stages of pregnancy; she was wearing a diaphanous dress, the size of her stomach was amazing.

'Those your Newport Menthols?' she asked Sparling, taking one.

'This your Busch beer?' She opened a can.

'Oh, by the way, Sparling, I hear your old lady thrown your ass out again.'

Princess had a habit of pronouncing each syllable as if she were reading aloud; this was intended to be ironic – and to emphasize the irony she sometimes made 'air quotes' by flashing two fingers on both hands while she spoke.

Sparling made a hissing noise – 'sheeee' – sinking back onto the sofa. 'I hear ...' pronounced Princess, pausing while Sparling went on hissing – 'sheeee' – as if to discourage her, '. . . I hear old Ronny Sue got herself a new beau; replace your ass, boy.'

Sparling was swatting an invisible fly.

Princess went on. 'I hear it's Happy Jack is Ronny Sue's new beau. He staying there at Cockerdoody's. Old Ronny Sue knows you're at Mary Alice's.'

Sparling pretended to aim a rifle at the fly, following it through the sights. Then he said, 'Happy Jack? He was born with a tail! Everybody knows he's sick in the head.'

Princess refuted this. 'Maybe Happy Jack didn't take to school. Don't mean he's stupid. Heck, I ain't stupid and I sure don't go.' She swung her dome around and walked away, very lightly, as if attached to a balloon, stage-whispering. 'Bye, you all.'

The senior executive of the Pirate's Cove consortium, Mr Advani, who had been stocking the deli counter with pickles and raw onion rings, came to the door. Princess barged past him contemptuously with a cold green stare and Mr Advani, watching her leave the store, sighed and wrinkled his brow with grave concern. Turning to Sparling, he enquired, 'Please, how is Mr Cockerdoody?'

Sparling was sitting down again, opening another beer. 'Cockerdoody, Cockerdoody, well, hell. He just 'bout dyin' there.'

'What are doctors saying?' enquired Mr Advani.

'They don't think that old boy gone make it, I reckon that's what I understand from what I'm bein' told; they don't say that, I mean, but that is what they implicatin'; they ain't quite sayin' it, they indicatin' . . .'

'Yes, yes, yes. Please. I understand. Have his family been notified?'

'Sounds to me like little shit-for-brains Happy Jack knows well enough. Sheeee.'

On my way back across the marsh I met Ronny Sue, who was livid with sunburn (even the crown of her head was burnt because her pale yellow hair was rather thin) and carrying a bottle of Wild Irish Rose. Ronny Sue had bulging blue eyes that contrasted strikingly with her red skin. I commented on her burn. Ronny Sue explained, 'Been fishin' with my boyfriend.'

'Did you catch anything?'

'Nothin' except a damn good buzz.'

Ronny Sue told very good stories. She told me, for instance, that an old man called Gokey had lived in a shack not far from the lighthouse. Gokey would have nothing to do with anybody. There was not even a path to the shack; you had to wade across the sodden ground.

Neighbours grew worried about him when he did not emerge from the shack for a couple of months. The doors and windows were locked from the inside. Health inspectors came over from Galveston and broke the door down.

Gokey was dead and, because the shack was so damp, his body had decomposed into a stinking mush. The inspectors found a tin box stuffed with banknotes, which they had to hang on a clothes line to dry. Then they burnt the shack with Gokey's remains inside it.

She also told me about the Cajuns who came down the peninsula in the late 1920s to work at a shrimp cannery on the bay-side tip; there were still a few houses there, known locally as Frenchtown.

One of the Cajuns, Lonnie Maturin, had a curse upon him; he was shadowed by a large white wolf. The wolf was reckoned to be the spirit of an insurance investigator Maturin had held underwater and drowned in the Bayou Teche. It was often seen slinking through the high salt grass. Cattle went missing. Sometimes people heard a mournful wail. Ronny Sue's own father had tried to shoot the creature but the bullets passed straight through its body. The wolf left the peninsula only when Maturin returned to Louisiana.

That morning Ronny Sue was in a bad mood and not very talkative. She had just had an argument with Mary Alice. 'Now I'm gone find me that scum-bucket Sparling.'

Sitting on the steps of the House of Blue Lights, beside Mary Alice and just above Lucilla, was a cheerful young man with a pink face and long brown hair, wearing baggy shorts and a Jack Daniels T-shirt. Lucilla had produced a reefer, which the pink-faced man was sharing.

Mary Alice was excited. 'Joseph, Joseph, this young man's Happy Jack. He's old Cockerdoody's grandson.'

I wondered if he really was born with a tail. Happy Jack smiled, focusing his gaze somewhere just beyond me. He described a circle with his right hand and drawled, 'Way.'

(Lucilla looked at me quizzically, smiling as if to say: 'Now, what do you make of him?' She often gave me little nudges, almost conspiratorial, implying that we were both onlookers.)

It was common knowledge that Cockerdoody was dying of tuberculosis. He lived in a big green house about half a mile down the road, behind the Horseshoe Liquor and Meat Mart.

Cockerdoody had been a successful shrimper, in that he had been able to make shrimping a lifetime's occupation. He was so old that he remembered fishing in Galveston Bay before it was polluted.

I never met Cockerdoody, because he was too ill to cope with newcomers, but his condition was the principal topic of conversation.

§

Near the House of Blue Lights there is a corner of land where the woman some historians call the Mother of Texas lived. The epithet displays a narrow homogenous view of history; although she was the first woman to arrive in the Spanish territory of Texas from the United States, there must have been any number of Indian and Mexican women there before her and no doubt their descendants are still in Texas; which is not to belittle her strength of character, her combination of tenacity and idealism.

Jane Wilkinson was born on 6 July 1798, at the Truman Place Plantation, on the Patuxent River in Maryland. In the same year her father, Captain Wilkinson, died. Jane and her mother lived at Truman Place for thirteen years before moving to live nearer Mrs Wilkinson's married daughter, Barbara Wilkinson Calvit, whose husband's plantation was called Propinquity because it was quite near Natchez in the Mississippi territory. Natchez was a wealthy, civilized place; fortunes were to be made there.

Mrs Wilkinson found a pleasant house in the settlement called Washington, and no sooner were she and Jane established than she fell down dead. So Jane, and her maid Kiamatia, moved to Propinquity to live with the Calvits.

The War of 1812 had been won at the Battle of New Orleans. Many of the injured victors recuperated at Natchez. Staying at Propinquity was Dr James Long, a hero of the battle, who had come to dress the wounds of his comrades.

Dr Long was handsome and brave but considered impulsive; he tended to get excited quickly. It was a temperament that Jane, a very self-possessed girl, found diverting. One evening she challenged him to a game of draughts. When Jane won, he presented her with a pair of chamois gloves, which she refused; so the doctor gave a shrill laugh and proposed marriage instead. Although she was only fourteen years old, Jane accepted.

Mrs Calvit, who was aghast, insisted upon a lengthy engagement (with the hope that her sister would recant) but Jane was adamant, as was Dr Long.

They were married at Propinquity on 14 May 1815.

For a while Dr Long practised medicine at Port Gibson, but Jane persuaded her husband that he should become a planter, so he bought a plantation called Walnut Hills, where their first child, Ann Herbert, was born in November 1816.

Walnut Hills was not a profitable venture. Within two years Dr Long sold the estate and moved to Natchez to become a merchant; that remained his occupation for the next two years.

In 1817 John Quincy Adams had signed a treaty that gave over the largely unoccupied territory of Texas to the Spanish, a gesture that infuriated the Mississippi settlers who saw westward expansion as their very destiny. Their sense of betrayal led to the notion of taking the territory by force.

The sum of $500,000 was raised by subscription, and an army was formed, with Dr Long as its general. Every volunteer, announced the new general, was to receive one league of Texas land.

Jane sewed a beautiful flag for the expedition, of white silk, striped and fringed in red, with a white star in the centre of a red ground in the upper distaff corner.

In June 1819 an advance force of 120 Mississippians crossed the Sabine River and reached the city of Nacogdoches. The citizens of Nacogdoches, who were not loyal to Spain, greeted the soldiers and a provisional government was set up at Camp Freeman; this was to be an Independent Republic of Texas with General Long as its president. The Lone Star flag was raised.

Meanwhile, back at Natchez, Jane had given birth to a second daughter and, although General Long had told his wife that he would send for her when things were settled, she took her maid Kiamatia and two-year-old Ann and the fortnight-old Rebecca and headed west to join the expedition.

Without any funds to speak of, the two women and the two infants travelled by boat to Alexandria, Louisiana, where the Calvits had recently moved from Propinquity. Jane then fell ill for a month and was unable to contact her husband, to let him know that she was about to join him.

To encourage more settlers to the republic, the Supreme Council of Texas was now offering each volunteer 6,400 acres and selling the meadowlands beside the Red River at less than 50 cents an acre.

Among those attracted to the offer were some men who agreed to escort Jane Long. She left Kiamatia and her daughters with Mrs Calvit and set off.

The First Lady of the Republic of Texas arrived to find her quarters not a governor's mansion but one room, in an eight-room blockhouse.

James Long had 300 men under his command but, for all the president's idealism and talk of liberty and the rights of man, most of the settlers were interested only in cheap land and often proved ungovernable. That very morning, he told Jane, he had been insulted by a drunk whom he had caught stealing a bottle of ink. 'The scoundrel would drink it.'

Despite the arrival of his wife, Long decided to travel to Galveston to enlist Jean Lafitte, his comrade at the Battle of New Orleans, whose navy was perceived by Long as a model of independent organization.

Lafitte was cynical about the Republic of Texas and its Supreme Council but happy to accept the title of Governor of Galveston Island. He presented the President of Texas with a yellow dog. Tied about its neck was a cotton handkerchief painted in approximation of the republic's flag.

Long declared Galveston a port of entry and authorized the building of a fort at Point Bolivar. The dog he named Galveston, after the historic meeting. But Long was not convinced by Lafitte, who seemed an unsound fellow.

One inconvenience was that the $500,000 appeared to be staying in Mississippi; the republic was short of funds. Long's men were forced to live off the land or buy what they could from Lafitte's navy, who stood by sneering at them.

Over the next year the grumbling settlers divided into isolated groups across southeastern Texas, where they were easily routed by the Spanish who had been informed, probably by Lafitte, of the invaders from Mississippi.

Long himself escaped capture by joining forces with a group of Mexican revolutionaries. He returned to supervise his retreating settlers and find his wife, and the two of them crossed the Sabine River and went back to Mrs Calvit's house in Alexandria.

There Jane discovered that Rebecca had died. Kiamatia told her that the baby had died within days of her departure. She insisted that Jane keep her and Ann with her always. 'I am your maid Kiamatia; where you go I will go and where you lodge I will lodge, and Ann is the daughter you carried.'

By April 1820 Long had returned to the fort at Bolivar and revived the Supreme Council with the Mexican revolutionaries. However, the two groups quickly fell out.

Long, still without adequate funds from Mississippi, struggled on with about eighty followers. Among them were Jane and Kiamatia and Ann, and by now there were two more women, also wives of doctors. These doctors' wives were cautious middle-class women who followed a line of pragmatism. The First Lady was more inspired by the heights of philosophy and courage. She found the women craven and dull. One was addicted to smelling salts. The other's Baptist orthodoxy annoyed Jane.

She preferred the wisdom of Kiamatia when it came to religious matters, for the maid was a visionary and a composer of hymns based on visions. Jane, who loved the Psalms and the Song of Solomon, chiefly for the poetry, encouraged Kiamatia's talent; she would adjust the scansion of a line here and there.

In the summer of the following year Jane announced that she was pregnant again. The doctors had appealed to her to wait until the colony was established. Their wives, who found Jane arrogant, were vexed at her for ignoring medical judgement.

In September 1821 Long sailed with fifty-two men to capture La Bahia. Although they managed to take the settlement, Spanish reinforcements soon appeared and Long and his men were imprisoned.

Back at Bolivar the remaining settlers, including the doctors and their wives, grew disconsolate and fled. Jane and Kiamatia and Ann chose to stay. 'My husband left me here and I shall stay until he returns.'

The last settler to leave took the rest of the provisions with him. The dog Galveston stayed with the women; he was loyal and unaware that dreadful hunger was ahead.

Jane was six months pregnant. Kiamatia was faithful but she wished that her mistress had left with the doctors and their wives as she had been urged to. Sometimes she wondered if the Longs' idealism was a kind of madness: watching their own reflections pass by in history – not vanity, but every movement engendered by the political thought behind it – instead of just moving and getting along as she did.

The reality of having nothing but a few fish-hooks and one line, a pair of muskets (that only Jane could use), a cannon (likewise), a limited amount of ammunition, and no food whatsoever, daunted Kiamatia, no matter how resolute her mistress.

They might have appealed to Lafitte for assistance, but they had seen the fire on the island, and the ships sailing away in all directions.

The Karankawas, subdued by Lafitte, had developed a reliance on European provisions; after the pirates left they were hungry again. They got into their rough-hewn canoes and rowed over to Bolivar to see if there was any food to be found.

The chief, a seven-foot giant, stood in his boat waving a damask table cloth; the others waved pots and pans. The women feared the Karankawas were coming to eat them and Jane fired the cannon. This initiated hostility and the Karankawas, who might have been helpful, were a persistent menace.

Jane, with her pair of muskets, provided sea-birds. Ann found birds' eggs. Kiamatia cast the fishing line and caught drum and snapper; extra fish were preserved in a barrel of brine that had once contained pickles. The abundance of oil in the livers of both fowl and fish gave the dog mange.

•

The final months of 1821 brought colder weather than the women had expected. Sweeps of green ice floated in the bay.

One morning Kiamatia observed a brown bear walking on the green ice; it was crossing the sea to Galveston. Kiamatia shouted to the bear, 'Come back! The Indians will eat you!' Presently she fell ill, becoming unconscious.

Kiamatia's fevers were sometimes so fierce that she steamed; then Jane and her daughter, wearing muslin masks, would lie beside her, and the dog lay across the feet of all three.

On the night of 21 December there was a blizzard, and Jane gave birth to her third daughter, Mary James. She wrapped the baby in muslin and held her against Kiamatia for several hours.

In the morning she laid Mary James in the arms of her maid and took Ann to search for food. The blizzard had frozen hundreds of fish: there were fish all over the strand. The pickle barrel was soon full. The dog gathered the frozen fish in his mouth, he made his own supply in a hole that he dug near the cabin; all the rest of that day he crept down to the windy shore to collect fish.

Kiamatia seemed more restful with Mary James in her arms; she remained unconscious but the fevers subsided.

The weather became milder after the blizzard. Jane had placed the pickle barrel outside the cabin and on Christmas Eve a herd of whooping cranes descended to steal the fish. Jane tried to scare them away; she was hesitant to fire the muskets, ammunition was running low.

The dog barked at the cranes, Jane shouted and Ann clapped.

Then Jane changed her mind about the musket but failed to bring down a single crane. Altogether there was such a disturbance that Kiamatia woke up. She announced that she had witnessed a series of marvellous visions: these were not of a mystical nature, they were to do with food.

By Christmas Day Kiamatia was able to walk. She went to the chest and unpacked a hammock that Jane had brought from Propinquity. Kiamatia had dreamt about using the hammock as a net. She went with Jane to the marsh and they trawled three mullet. The catch also corresponded with Kiamatia's vision.

The mullet were to be used as bait, for a great big fish that had swum into Kiamatia's dream when she was ill. The dream fish would be big enough to feed them for a couple of weeks, and Kiamatia knew exactly where to catch it.

They set off to a sand-bar on the southern shore. Kiamatia was the more skilful angler but Jane insisted that, if the fish was as big as Kiamatia reckoned, it would require her strength to pull it in.

Kiamatia argued that it was not a matter of strength but of knowing the fish.

Jane said that she would follow Kiamatia's directions, and took the line and tied it around her waist.

Kiamatia told her that tying the line around her waist was wrong to begin with: the fish would pull her into the sea.

Jane argued that if the fish was too strong for her alone, Kiamatia could hold on to her, so that the fish would be pulling against both their weights.

Kiamatia told her that it didn't work that way; she implored Jane to let her catch the fish as she had done in her dream.

'Enough of your dream,' snapped Jane and hurled the line out.

Within minutes there was a great tug and Jane was dragged off the sand-bar. She managed to break herself free. Both women saw a huge tarpon leap out of the surf, with their only fishing line in its mouth.

Fortunately Kiamatia had dreamt about an oyster-bed as well.

Two days after Christmas, a ship passed and two men rowed ashore. They were from Monterey and they brought a letter stating that General Long was alive but a prisoner working in a silver mine. The men handed the letter to Jane and immediately rowed back to their ship.

January was a long, hopeless month. Apart from the oysters, most of Kiamatia's other visions proved false. Eventually the women ate what they could of the fish that the dog had buried.

They accepted the possibility of starvation.

Kiamatia gave up talking; she gathered driftwood, or she sat in the dunes watching the horizon and banging a toy drum that one of the settlers had made for Ann. Jane found Kiamatia's silence and moody drumming dispiriting.

One day, towards the end of the month, Jane heard her maid screaming. She rushed to the dunes and found her pointing eastward along the strand. Three men, who were neither Indians nor Mexicans, were running away. Jane ran after them, calling for them to wait, but the three men went faster and faster and were soon out of sight.

Trudging back towards the fort, Jane saw a string caught in some weed; the string ran into the sea. Jane thought it might be used as a fishing line and, picking the string up, realized that it was indeed a fishing line. Furthermore, as she gathered the line in, it became clear that a fish of some size was attached to the other end. So Jane hauled and hauled and brought in the tarpon that had been lost on Christmas Day.

Two days later Kiamatia screamed again. Ships were passing. Jane and Kiamatia and Ann waved frantically but the ships sailed on. Jane fired the cannon. The ships anchored and a sloop put out with fifteen men aboard.

The ships carried the first of Stephen F. Austin's colonists (the Old Three Hundred, who would prove a better organized, more determined force than the Mississippians). The new colonists had been told that the fort at Bolivar was completely abandoned. Among the men aboard the sloop were the three who had run away from Jane; they had come ashore to investigate the ruins of the fort and they had mistaken the drumming, screeching Kiamatia for a Karankawa.

The colonists were sailing to two destinations: a site at the mouth of the Brazos river, and the Matamoros settlement at the mouth of the Rio Grande. They offered to take the women and children with them but Jane refused. She would wait for her husband as she had arranged. Kiamatia wept quietly. The dog snarled at anyone who went near him. Some of the men returned to the ships to collect provisions and ammunition for the women; others formed a hunting party and supplied meat.

That night the vessels moored in the bay. The next morning they sailed on down the coast.

A couple of days later more visitors arrived: a man named James Smith, whom Jane had met before at Calcasieu in Louisiana, was rowing a *pirogue* loaded with his belongings; his wife and children walked along the beach. Smith had long admired Jane's bravery; he promised that once he was settled in Texas he would send supplies to the women. Then he elected to leave his fifteen-year-old daughter, Peggy, so that she could tell her future offspring of her association with the historic women. These were people for whom the claiming of one's place in history was as urgent as the claiming of land.

Word spread about the women on the peninsula. One day the captain of a ship from New Orleans stopped to tell Jane that he had news of her husband: Long had been released from prison but was negotiating a land agreement with the authorities in Mexico City, and that could take as long as a year. The ship was headed for Matamoros; the captain offered to take Jane and Kiamatia and Peggy and the children with him and promised that he would pay for their passage on to Mexico City.

Jane accepted the offer but asked the captain to return Peggy to her family should they pass them *en voyage*. The women and the dog Galveston spent that night aboard the anchored ship.

In the morning another ship from New Orleans arrived, with more recent news of General Long: he was about to leave Mexico after all and would be sailing, any day, from Veracruz. Jane and her entourage immediately disembarked, to continue waiting as before. Both ships sailed away.

In the middle of March, James Smith rowed back to Bolivar to collect his daughter, bringing the promised supplies. Peggy urged Jane and Kiamatia to come to her family's new base, across Galveston Bay at

San Jacinto. James Smith assured them that there was room in the *pirogue*.

Jane regarded the Smiths as like-minded people and decided that her husband would easily be able to find her with them and, to Kiamatia's delight and relief, she agreed. Off they all set in the *pirogue*, the dog following along the shore. Everyone was high-spirited.

At a settlement called Rankins, not far from the Smiths' home, the women came across the first fresh water they had tasted in months.

Galveston drank so much that he became bloated and died. He was buried on Smith's land. In his honour Jane recited the 19th Psalm. When questioned on her selection by Mrs Smith, she replied that the dog had often wagged his tale to the words of the Bible and to that psalm especially. Such profanity irritated Mrs Smith. When Kiamatia extemporized an elegy, much of it wordless ululation, Mrs Smith was appalled.

Other colonists at San Jacinto told Jane that her husband's return had been delayed. A trader called Terrill, on his way to Matamoros, promised Jane that he would ascertain the situation and write back to her.

In the meantime Jane and Kiamatia and Ann and Mary stayed with the Smith family. Life was not very pleasant, as Jane and Mrs Smith disagreed upon most things. James Smith caught a fever and Jane, insisting that she was a doctor's wife, wanted to nurse him. Mrs Smith was indignant and nursed him herself. James Smith grew more and more ill while the women squabbled; finally he died.

Jane and Kiamatia and the children moved to Rankins, where an old black man built them a hut of boards and palmetto leaves. The old man had a cow and supplied them with milk; a doctor called Jeter would sell them meat for 50 cents a pound, and occasionally they were brought venison.

Kiamatia taught Ann to fish in the little bayou.

Jane wrote to Mrs Calvit, but no reply came, and constantly she waited for word from Terrill.

Two brothers, Randal and Jimmy Jones, who had been among

General Long's original settlers, recognized their erstwhile First Lady in her reduced circumstances. The Jones brothers built Jane a comfortable cabin, near their own, at Tuscoseta Crossing on the Trinity River. Some embarrassment arose when the brothers, believing that Jane must have some money, asked for $100 in payment.

At Tuscoseta Crossing, Jane finally received a letter from Terrill:

> Genl. Long was well recd. in Mexico [City] & had recd. several visits together with many invitations from our English Col., one of which he was about to return, when he was hailed by a Centinel and ordered to stop, at the same time, Genl. Long put his hand to his side pocket to draw a paper [his passport]. The Centinel supposing it to be for the purpose of drawing his side fire arms to defend himself, at which time the Centinel fired at Genl. Long; and the ball entered his side & passed thro' him; he expired in a few minutes. His death was much regretted by the inhabitants in general. The Congress have it in contemplation, as soon as they get through the hurry of business as respects the Govt., to make a hansome appropriation for yours & childred & support. Mr. Sulivan gives the above statements in the presence of those whom accompanied him, and was at the interment, which was attended with a great concourse of people, exclusive of 40 coaches and that every respect was paid. He was not buried with the honors of war in consequence of his not being a Catholic.

Terrill went on to say that José Trespalacios, the Mexican Governor of Texas, was in San Antonio, and that it was to Trespalacios that Jane should apply for the pension that the Mexican government, regretful that Long had been murdered in the midst of diplomatic negotiations, were settling. Jane sent the governor a letter immediately.

She also heard from her sister in Alexandria, who sent her a slave called Tom and a mule.

Trespalacios wrote back that he was reluctant to send money through such unstable territory. Jane exchanged a set of silver spoons, that had been a wedding present, for a horse to ride and on 9 September 1822 she set off for San Antonio. The Jones brothers, still eager to be paid for the cabin, agreed to escort her. The cavalcade included Jane's daughters and Kiamatia and Tom and two other slaves belonging to the brothers. It took five weeks to reach San Antonio.

Jane called upon the Baron de Bastrop, to whom she had a letter of introduction. (The *soi-disant* Baron was actually a fugitive Dutch embezzler called Bogel; his unquestioned nobility made him respectable in the New World; he served as a judge and sat on the city council.) Bastrop accompanied Jane to the governor's mansion.

Trespalacios extended every courtesy but announced that the Mexican government was disputing Jane's right to a pension. Jane resolved to stay in San Antonio until the matter was settled.

The Jones brothers complained so Jane gave them the slave Tom, and the horse, and the mule.

Then she settled down to wait for the money. For six months Jane and Kiamatia lived peacefully in San Antonio as guests of the Government. Mary James was baptized there and Ann attended school. Political turmoil in Mexico greatly confused the issue. Trespalacios fled to Monterey. The pension looked increasingly unlikely.

A merchant from Philadelphia, Leonard Peck, was organizing a train of forty mules to New Orleans; Jane agreed to return with Peck to the United States. The train reached the banks of the Brazos, where an old widowman feasted the travellers on water-melons. When the lonely old man discovered Jane's identity he dropped to his knees. 'The Lord has sent you to ease my seniority. Marry me, I beseech you, Mrs Long.' Jane, of course, refused.

Alexander Calvit, her brother-in-law, met the mule train near Nacogdoches and took Jane and Kiamatia and his nieces to Alexandria.

The Mexican government never granted Jane's pension. She spent the next few years as a member of the Calvit household.

In 1824 the Calvits left Alexandria for Texas, where they struggled to make a living farming beside the Neches, but, two years running, their crops failed.

Little Mary James (the first American to be born in Texas) died of herpetic fever, from a single blister on her lip.

In 1831 Ann was married, and the next year Jane and Kiamatia took to running a boarding-house in Brazoria.

Jane's reputation as the former First Lady made the house a sought-after accommodation in the days, after the War of Independence, when Texas was a republic again. David Burnet, Sam Houston and Mirabeau Lamar, the first three presidents of the new republic, all stayed at Jane's boarding-house.

In 1837, when she was thirty-nine years old she moved to some farmland that had been granted to her by the republic. The land at Richmond, in Fort Bend County, was good and Jane prospered; by 1850 her plantation was valued at more than $10,000. By the time the Civil War began, Jane was known to all of Texas as Grandma Long, and she was fiercely loyal to the South. She would buy nothing that was produced in the North and expounded the virtues of self-sufficiency: she wore dresses made of cotton grown on her own plantation and wove a wide-brimmed hat from palmetto leaves; she produced all her own food and smoked a corn-cob pipe of her own tobacco.

Jane Long died at Richmond on 30 December 1880. Kiamatia died shortly afterwards.

Although Mary Alice lived less than a quarter of a mile from where the women spent their lonely winter, she had never heard of them. Nor had Lucilla. The only person familiar with the story was Ronny Sue – but she believed that the women starved to death and that their skeletons were discovered by subsequent settlers. Fort Travis, now a park of no great charm, was built on the site of the earlier fort. I would go there to watch ships.

Three

LEANING ON THE RAIL AT THE STERN OF THE FERRY, I HOPED FOR dolphins. I had seen them at the mouth of Galveston Bay before. Porpoises, too, will enter the bay, and the giant rays called devil-fish (some measuring 14 feet in wingspan and weighing as much as 2,000 lbs) and immense sawfish (*Pristiophori*) of a similar weight, have been caught in these waters. Dark green jew-fish (the biggest can reach 700 lbs) swim quite near the shore.

The sea can still produce monsters: in 1887 a fisherman was towed two miles by a 'Granduquois', an unclassified fish of prehistoric mien, six foot long with an alligator's jaws. In 1951 a shrimp boat brought in a 2,000-lb leatherback turtle.

There are sharks but attacks on humans are rare. In 1976 a 14-foot Tiger Shark, caught off Galveston, was found to have a human skull in its stomach. In 1983 a windsurfer disappeared. Later a leg washed up at Corpus Christi; it was still wearing a Nike trainer. The board was found thirty miles out into the gulf.

Gulls swooped and screamed. The sea air was tainted by the chain-smoker standing beside me, a man so agitated that I thought he might jump overboard.

'Question marks continually assault my persona, you know what I mean? Should I be doubtful?'

The man was in his forties, not a Texan, not even a Southerner, but down from New Jersey; a light-skinned black man with fast, almost Chinese eyes, wearing a child's Olive Oyl T-shirt pulled up high over his lean stomach (which he had scratched until red welts rose up). He had been the last motorist to roll on.

His car was a brown Volkswagen Rabbit with a crumpled bonnet – a snarling Rabbit. On the passenger seat was a stack of boards, wrapped loosely in newspaper. There had been a fire on the back seat, the upholstery was eaten away.

Henry Glover smelt of seaweed. He had spent the previous night in Beaumont, having sold blood plasma in the afternoon. 'I lack the time and, to be straight with you, the do-re-mi to keep my presentation up sufficiently for the interview possibility. I am an artist; that does not take qualification. Either the work itself holds . . .'

His speech meandered. Words tumbled and jumbled in such an erratic torrent that to contain a single phrase, even to answer a question, required an effort he clearly found exhausting. Whenever he opened his mouth you could hear the churning of his mind. He showed me a small crumpled card that read HENRY GLOVER, ARTIST.

I asked about the pictures. 'Flowerings, brother. Painterly abstraction. Drawing from the inner mirror, forging harmonies. All the pictures are based on visions and what I am shown by God. I call them flowerings. I see domes and chandeliebras and natural shapes curling. They are all stowed just now. But . . .' he paused to emit a cloud of stale smoke '. . . without the chance to exhibit, how am I going to spread the word?'

He was hoping to solve the problem in Texas. Henry Glover read aloud from a typed list. 'In Galveston: Conrad Contemporary, Dutchman, Galerie D'Alexandria, Gallery 2211 . . .' He was heading back towards the Rabbit. 'You need a ride someplace?' I thanked him but I was happy to walk.

I sauntered off the ferry, past avenues named after fish (Pompano, Marlin, Albacore, Bonita), until I was close to the UTMB campus. Then I strolled down Sixth Street to Seawall Boulevard.

On the beach stood two hydraulic cranes. One had a cable hanging from it and at the end of the cable was a harness. People could be fastened into the harness, then be hooked onto a chain from the other crane and hoisted up. At the top of the second crane they were unhooked to swing out across the beach, attached to the cable, flying backwards and forwards like Peter Pan. It was a variant of bungy-jumping.

The cranes were only used at weekends. It was a weekday and the beach was almost deserted. I stood looking at the cranes and a young black man (with hair like a pillbox hat) rode up on a bicycle. He announced, 'They can't pay me enough to go on that thing!' I said that I wouldn't do it either. He added, 'You got to watch out below. They always shittin' themselves.'

Then he said, 'You should have been here with the beach whale. Jesus, they smell *bad*,' and rode away, which was frustrating because I am interested in beached whales.

In 1916 two Galveston workmen captured a 60-foot Atlantic right whale, brought in by a storm and evidently injured. Most of the time it was docile; intermittently it thrashed in agony. The workmen towed the whale to the docks, where they covered it with a canvas tarpaulin and charged spectators 10 cents. If the whale was asleep they would prod it with the handle of a spade. The whale died a slow obscene death, and was dissected: it was miraculous that the whale had survived the storm at all, since most of the bones in its body were broken; it was unfortunate to have entered show business in such condition.

•

Henry Glover's Rabbit had made it off the ferry but conked out within minutes on the island. He wasn't far from the parking area on Porretto Beach. I offered to push him there.

The car, despite containing his every possession, was light and free-moving. Henry Glover looked about, squinting in the glare. 'Guess this is where I stay. Maybe there won't be no hit-the-road-jackies, that it is to be hoped. If they ain't got no chocolate yoohoo in heaven, excuse me, but I'll go through hell.'

'Can I see the pictures?'

'You think you interested?'

'Possibly. I haven't got much money.'

'Brother, did I mention transaction of any kind? *Interested* is what I asked.'

He unwrapped a parcel of boards. They were indeed strange, and flowerings would be an appropriate description. Most seemed to be chalk patterns on a dark background, as if miraculous fireworks, more ornamental than any I had ever seen, were exploding in a night sky. Visionary pavement art. 'A drum beats in the centre of my skull,' explained Henry Glover.

I was impressed. There was a sort of folk mysticism, a Hindu quality (the intricate *rangoli* patterns drawn on thresholds) to the pictures. Now I saw Henry Glover as a sadhu in a benighted land.

'You could sell these,' I told him. 'You might have to find a gallery that shows naïve art . . .'

'God ain't naïve,' muttered Henry Glover, lighting a cigarette.

'Why don't you display them on the street somewhere? You could make a living. And maybe gather some attention from an established gallery.'

'Brother, I am passing through this world without wealth, the Lord having seen fit to shape me as a Afro-American from the urban proletariat. In the streets of the cities I am next to unseen. Without wealth, I am bound to work for piss-ant money and what do I get? I tell you what I have got. A unique facility. I am God's feedpipe . . .' his face was momentarily lost in smoke . . . 'and the value of that divine throughput is beyond estimation. You ever hear about Lorenzo Medici? They called him magnificent. Somewhere in the United States, brother, I'm going to find me a patron. Texas got to be a richness centre. See, selling these don't interest me as much as showing them to the people. Education, spiritualization, enlightenmentation. Somebody come along and slap down a annuity, that enable me to work undisturbanced . . . on the condition that I show I am working . . . show and share . . . till that time I can live. I got the white blood cells, they are like gold inside my body. I got food past its date, every supermarket in America. I ain't going to starve.'

I went to Speedy Gonzales, a Mexican restaurant, where, many years ago, Nadia had waited tables. I could picture her then: in her teens she had a Joan of Arc look and her short hair swung like a curved copper blade; carrying food, she must have resembled a page in a Norman castle.

Nadia lives in San Francisco now and makes a living as a photographer. She has remarried; her husband is a Japanese country-and-western singer called Kenzaburo 'Jimmy' Yoshiwara. In Tokyo he led a rockabilly band called the Burning Monsters (their one hit was 'I am a Burning Fireman'). Nadia met Jimmy in 1986 when the Burning Monsters toured the roadhouses and dance-halls of Texas and Louisiana; she took some photographs that were published in *Texas Monthly*. In California Jimmy pursues a solo career, performing his own songs and covering Bakersfield classics by Skeets McDonald and Buck Owens. By all accounts he is very talented; he plays to a young sophisticated crowd but he is not accepted by the mainstream country-and-western audience. Nadia and Jimmy have two young sons, called Jerry Lee and Duane.

For years we didn't communicate but now we are friends again, across the world. Some of our conversations are strained. When I told Nadia I was going back to Galveston, she said she wasn't surprised. 'I know you were kinda drawn to it down there. Just make sure you can leave. You know, people get trapped.' I wanted her to go on (the notion of Galveston as Circe's island was interesting) but she changed the focus. 'I guess you are more interested in examining life than living.'

Speedy Gonzales is run by Mr Mendoza, a portly sea-lion of a man with a bald head and a pencil moustache. He is also known as El Gran Queso, the Originator of the Pumpkin Seed Salad.

Mr Mendoza seems constantly to be muttering but actually he has a patter; it is almost inaudible and based upon vintage radio comedy routines. Mr Mendoza did some broadcasting in the services in the 1950s – 'I coulda given it a shot, sure' – but he found success in the restaurant business.

'Sure I remember Nadia. She had that mother from Poland or somewhere, some kinda babushka.' Mr Mendoza then took up a patter on a Russian theme (it might have been from a Marx Brothers original).

Speedy Gonzales is well placed, just above the beach. You can buy a colour photograph of Mr Mendoza in pirate fancy dress for $50, a framed version for $70. The photograph is inscribed *Good wishes, El Gran Queso*. Mr Mendoza interrupted the patter to tell me that it was a joke. 'People like the joke. Hey, I musta sold three or four, unframed.'

The food on the breakfast menu was very expensive, I suppose because one ate looking out to sea – equally, the cheaper food available nearby was straightforward junk, so the leap in price signified quality – but I kept wondering if $5 for *huevos rancheros* was another joke. That was $5 for two eggs and a dab of refried beans and a splash of *picante* sauce. Flour tortillas, potatoes and coffee were extra. 'Who says you gotta eat here?' I went to a table anyway.

My waitress, whose name was Vanessa, was in her forties; her hair was dyed blue-black and she had long red nails that were a little bestial. She was once employed as a lighting technician at Pinewood Studios. Vanessa was awash with London memories: Kensington Market, Princess Anne's wedding and Santana at the Rainbow.

'You ever read anything by Tom Beale-Davis?'

He used to be her boyfriend. I didn't recognize the name.

'He's a poet. He's kinda the Carlos Santana of poetry.'

*

I walked a long way down Seawall Boulevard. The sea was silvery brown and the sand was much the same colour. I passed a series of rock piers, jetties made of granite blocks, sometimes there were anglers on them.

Once Nadia and I had fished for crabs from one of these piers, using string and chicken necks. We put the crabs we caught in a styrofoam ice chest. On our way back to La Marque, the crabs dug a hole through the lid and crawled about on the back seat of the Belvedere. We had not counted them, we never knew if we found them all.

I remembered one of the piers strewn with pink-fleshed grapefruit, most of them squashed but some whole and edible. It looked as if somebody had deliberately pelted the pier from a boat. Nadia said the grapefruit reminded her of abortions; this mournful little comment fluttered in the salt air. Probably the grapefruit fell from a passing ship and dashed on the hard granite.

I thought about Nadia's mother, Misia, and the castaway life she must have led to end up in a small (predominantly working-class) town in Texas; an eccentric, helpless outsider who spoke three languages fluently but made a living cleaning offices. As a girl she had been introduced to Mr and Mrs Nabokov.

Nadia's father, Bob Williams, a merchant seaman, disappeared in 1964. Misia grew fat with loneliness, the floor of the Belvedere was always strewn with candy wrappers, and for some reason she walked about dressed in green hospital scrubs.

Her appearance suggested the European Avant-Garde of the 1920s – one could imagine her in cahoots with Tristan Tzara. In fact, artistically she was very pedestrian. She decorated the walls of her ugly little house with murals, imaginary Mediterranean landscapes in a fauvist style, the paint squeezed directly onto the wall and spread by palette knife – this made the rooms seem even smaller. She put candles in Chianti bottles; it was like a trattoria too untidy for customers.

Misia died of cancer, a few years after Nadia and I had separated. She had moved to an apartment in Houston.

Nadia told me that her mother likened the illness to having a black stocking caught in her throat; sometimes the stocking would unroll for a moment, then bunch up again.

I felt guilty that I had never befriended Misia and I hated to think of her death by strangulation; I tried retroactive prayer.

□ □

A large pleasure pier, built of iron and wood, with Polynesian-looking buildings on it, was for sale. Hardly anyone was about; it was very sleepy. Most of the businesses were motels and food outlets – all chains and franchises – and more souvenir shops. I turned up 37th Street, then cut diagonally backwards to Rosenberg Avenue which is 25th Street, passing the monument to the Battle of San Jacinto.

Galveston became a city when Michel Branamour Menard, a Canadian who had made a fortune trading with the Indians, bought a large tract of land from Juan Seguin of San Antonio, who had been granted the eastern end of the island by the Mexican government.

Menard, who recognized that Galveston Bay provided a fine natural harbour, owned the land when Texas became a republic in 1836. There were seven houses on the island by 1837. In 1838 Menard organized the Galveston City Company to sell lots.

The following year an Irishman called Francis Sheridan, working for the British Foreign Office, complained that the new town was 'singularly dreary', inhabited by a thousand drunken men wearing coats made out of blankets, who picked their teeth with knife-blades and spat incessantly. Such streets as existed were squalid.

The national anthem of Texas seemed to be 'Will You Come To The Bower', a tune whistled ubiquitously that irritated the Irishman.

Galveston grew rapidly. By 1840 there were 600 houses on the island and a population of nearly 4,000. A visitor called Charles Hooton wrote, in 1841:

> From the sea, the appearance of Galveston is that of a fine city of great extent, built close upon the edge of the water; but its glory vanishes gradually in proportion to the nearness of the approach of the spectator. He finds nothing but a poor straggling collection of weather-boarded frame houses, beautifully embellished with whitewash (they may be mistaken for white marble from the Gulf), and extending without measurable depth, about the length of two miles of string.

Entering Galveston Bay was hazardous, for the waters of the Gulf are shallow and the floor irregular; sand-bars shift constantly. Hooton describes the bay:

> Sprinkled with wrecks of various appearances and sizes – all alike gloomy, however, in their looks and associations – it strikes the heart of the stranger as a sort of ocean cemetery, a sea churchyard, in which broken masts and shattered timbers, half-buried in quicksands, seem to remain above the surface of the treacherous waters only to remind the living, like dead camels on a level desert, of the destruction that has gone before.

There were continual efforts to deepen the port, to dig channels that would enable larger ships to use the wharves on the bay side of the island.

Initially the larger ships anchored in the gulf and were unloaded by stevedores who sailed out on lighters. Even ships that could enter the bay found the waters too shallow to dock and many passengers were carried ashore on the backs of sailors.

The transition from sail to steam made the deepening even more necessary; it was not entirely satisfactory until the 1890s.

In October 1896 the world's largest cargo ship, the British steamer *Algoa*, could safely enter the bay.

Galveston's economy was based on port activities; it served as a storage and shipping point. River steamers carried cotton from southeast Texas to the island, where merchants compressed the loose bales with steam presses, then shipped it to New Orleans, New York and Europe.

Goods unloaded in Galveston were carried across the bay to Houston and distributed about the state. The city became the largest in Texas and a great optimism settled.

In 1845 Galveston was the first city in Texas with a chamber of commerce. By the end of that year the Republic of Texas was annexed by the United States. In 1846 A. Suthron, in his book *Prairiedom*, remarked

> Galveston, like Tyre, is built upon an island in the midst of the sea, and if her people, like the Tyrians of old, continue to be economical, industrious, and enterprising; sincere, faithful, and hospitable to strangers; if they maintain a good police, free trade, and are faithful to their engagements; if they punish fraud and reward virtue; if they are not inflated by avarice and pride on the one hand, nor enervated by luxury and idleness on the other; she will become the centre of commerce, the resort of all nations, and attain the wealth and power, and it may be, as we have elsewhere predicted, the greatness and glory of the ancient city.

All through the nineteenth century it was the point of entry for goods shipped into the state, as well as for European immigrants, bound for what was then the western frontier of America. Pelican Island, directly opposite the docks, was the Gulf Coast equivalent of Ellis Island.

The majority of immigrants who settled in Galveston were of German origin. By the 1850s half the population was German and Galveston had a German newspaper, *Die Union*. European shipowners encouraged migrants to arrive there because they could load up with the profitable Texas cotton for their trip back.

Cotton as an industry was dependent upon slavery. The importation of African slaves had been banned since 1808. The Mexican government forbade the importation of Caribbean slaves. The Republic of Texas allowed and encouraged slavery but it was difficult to obtain sufficient slaves to support the cotton industry.

There had always been some smuggling to meet the need. By the time Galveston was booming in the 1850s, slave smuggling had increased dramatically. The number of slaves in the state rose from 58,000 to 182,000.

Many were brought from other southern states but certainly thousands more were smuggled in from Africa by disreputable slave traders who landed on the beaches around Galveston.

It was estimated that healthy Africans cost the traders about $110 each – that figure includes the bribes paid to the British frigates patrolling the West African coast – but they could be sold for $1,000. It was difficult to prevent such a lucrative enterprise.

In 1858 an American ship, the *Thomas Watson*, with a female captain, Mrs Mattie Watson, arrived in Galveston with a cargo of eighty-nine camels. It wasn't the cargo that drew attention – there was an army camel corps based in the hill country; camels were used for exploring the desert. It was the way that the ship crept so slowly along the Gulf Coast that had aroused the suspicion of the British consul, who kept a closer eye on the illegal slave trade than any local authority would.

When she reached Galveston the camels were turned loose on the island and the *Thomas Watson* headed for Havana, a well-known slave centre. Realizing that she was being followed by a British schooner, Mrs Watson weighed anchor and, with all her crew, jumped overboard.

The ship then exploded, several barrels of gunpowder having been ignited with fuses. Whether a cargo of slaves was aboard remains uncertain; nor do we know if the captain and crew were far enough from the blast to survive; they were not captured.

The streets in the middle of the century were wide, boarded each side by sewage ditches. Vicious dogs – and enormous pigs, with neither tails nor ears – roamed freely about. However prosperous the port was, it was still a smelly, rough place to live. Fresh water was not supplied until the 1890s, when it was piped across the bay from Alta Loma on the mainland.

Mosquitoes swarmed and there were regular epidemics of yellow fever from 1839 to 1873. As much as a tenth of the city's population could perish, after vomiting black bile. Nobody had made the connection between the insects and the disease. 'Yellow Jack' was believed to be brought on by hot weather. Treatment was therefore ineffectual, consisting of mustard baths and stomach plasters. The worst epidemic hit the city during 1866 and 1867, claiming 1,150 victims at the rate of twenty a day. Describing the pestilence, in his admirable history of Galveston, David McComb writes:

> Burning tar fumigated the air of the city, grass filled with small green frogs grew rank on the Strand, and ringing of church bells for the deceased was so constant that it irritated the sick and living.

When the disease returned to the island in 1870 many citizens panicked and fled to the mainland. A trainload of refugees was met by an armed militia at Houston and sent back to the island.

During the Civil War, Galveston was blockaded by the Union navy. Union troops captured the port in 1862, but the Confederates took it back in a famous victory; they retained the city until the end of the war. The blockade, however, remained and the citizens, protected by the formidable General Magruder, endured harsh conditions.

The Confederate soldiers, essentially surrounded, were restless; some ransacked stores, and many deserted, but Magruder handed the port over only when news reached him of Lee's surrender.

On 5 June 1865 the flag of the United States was raised over the customs house, and the city, which had reached a level of some desolation, began to recover immediately.

After the war Galveston flourished again and great buildings went up. The domestic architecture is described as Victorian but it is quite unlike the Victorian architecture of Britain. I think what Americans call Victorian implies much filigree and gingerbread. Many of the larger buildings in Galveston have a Teutonic, Brothers Grimm quality.

The architect Nicholas Clayton designed over two hundred of them, commercial, municipal and residential; more than anyone Clayton is responsible for the appearance of the city that was called the Queen of the Gulf.

Tourists started to arrive, attracted by the beaches. Swimsuits, worn by both sexes, were made of flannel, moreen or serge; any stiff fabric that would not cling when wet. Conventions were held: the Missouri Valley Press Association arrived in 1875, the Texas Democratic Convention in 1876.

In 1891 there was a fat man's convention. At the time, obese men gathered in every American city to form fraternities with names like the Phorty Phunny Phellows and the Phiphteen Phigures of Phun (the *Phs* were for elephantine effect). To be overweight was not shameful, it was to be jolly and splendid. The fat men paraded in fine livery and raised money for charities; the Galveston convention was a magnificent occasion.

Clayton's grandest building, the Beach Hotel, was built in 1882 at a cost of $260,000. It stood on the beach, upon 300 cedar piles driven into the sand. It was three storeys high, with 200 bedrooms, opening onto verandahs and loggias. More or less the shape of a letter E, the Beach Hotel gave the impression of being three ornate pavilions, the central one beneath a bulbous octagonal dome. The building was mostly wooden and painted mauve. The eaves and gables were picked out with green and gold and the dome was striped red and white. On 22 July 1898, it burnt to the ground.

Clayton's remaining buildings reflect a slow pacific bourgeoisie; the solid houses rest among the palms and oleanders of their gardens as if napping through the hot afternoons.

Nicholas Clayton met a bizarre end: in 1916 he caught fire inspecting a crack in a chimney.

I watched a dignified old woman taking photographs of the exterior of the Bishop's Palace. She was wearing a wide-brimmed planter's panama and all her clothes were pressed with mathematical precision. She handled the camera with gloved hands. I guessed that the house had some family association for her. She embodied, in human form, many of its qualities: an ornate but tidy grandeur, seniority, and resistance to the climate and the changing times.

The building I like most in Galveston, the Sacred Heart Church at 14th and Broadway, is not designed by Clayton, although he had designed an earlier church on the site. It is a strange pale Saracenic building with a great white dome, on top of which stands a statue of the Christ of the Andes.

In 1875 Madame Rentze's Female Minstrels, a troupe of can-can dancers, performed at the Opera House. After the Female Minstrels left, olive oil and incense were burned to purify the theatre's atmosphere. The following year a knife-thrower, ('The Distinguished Culterjectionist') Madame Zarabanda (who was in fact a Welsh woman, Janet Ridley from Porthcawl), horrified a large audience by accidentally slicing the edge of a volunteer's ear. The bleeding man was escorted from the stage; Madame Zarabanda blithely called for another volunteer who would not flinch.

In the winter of 1879 Buffalo Bill's Wild West Show came to the island. There were freak shows and prize-fights, parachutists and sword swallowers to entertain the populace.

On 19 June 1882, Oscar Wilde arrived to give a lecture at the Pavilion. His subject was Beauty. Wilde was touring the United States to help promote Gilbert and Sullivan's 'Patience'; it was felt that theatregoers would better appreciate the satire if they had seen an aesthete for themselves.

Wilde appeared in sky-blue velvet breeches and a shirt frilled with lace. His hair was long and he carried a lily.

The audience consisted chiefly of women who longed for a less provincial existence. The men who attended were on guard, resentful of Smart Alecs.

The lecture did not go well. First of all an electric circuit broke, plunging the hall into darkness – it could have been worse: the next year faulty wiring burnt the Pavilion down altogether. When the lights came back on, Wilde was heckled by the men. His voice was faint and quavery and easily drowned.

The next day an anonymous critic wrote in the *Galveston Daily News*:

> The æsthete does not impress one as, except in the oddity of his dress, being a whit more worthy attention than the most ordinary looking man on the street. While the self-nominated head of the school of the beautiful he can not be considered as especially possessed of a spare supply of that article in his physical appearance. A poor delivery, an awkward manner, and a subject not broadly popular, are elements that will cause the brightest and purest language to fall flat on the general public.

In 1888 Lily Langtry arrived in a private railway carriage. Four years later Sarah Bernhardt performed *Tosca* and *Camille*. The most popular play of 1893 was the drag classic *Charley's Aunt*.

A few days before Christmas in 1907 a tall stout woman strode into a saloon on the Strand and threatened to smash every bottle in the building. In a booming voice, she harangued the patrons, 'Men, you ought not to drink that stuff! It will ruin your livers and damn your souls!' The belligerent woman was Carrie Nation, the most notorious temperance campaigner in America. Mrs Nation came from Brazoria County, quite near the island. Her husband, David Nation, an attorney, was an alcoholic who could not support his wife and retarded daughter. Mrs Nation ran a hotel in Richmond for several years, but her fierce piety and frightening temper repelled guests. When her husband died she moved to Kansas, where she embarked on a one-woman crusade against the demon drink.

Mrs Nation believed in direct action; she would personally smash every bottle she came across. This earned her some celebrity. From the late 1880s she was known as the Hatchet Lady.

An incredibly strong woman, she could tear the lead door of an icebox off its hinges and hurl a cash register across a room. She was impervious to broken glass: if necessary she would barge straight through a saloon window to make a dramatic entrance.

Mrs Nation was arrested in twenty-five states. She paid her legal fees by selling souvenir hatchets, giving lectures (encouraging audiences to follow her example) and publishing a newspaper called *The Hatchet*.

Her visit to Galveston was relatively peaceful: she gave a well-attended lecture, bawling down hecklers, then toured the saloons frightening the drinkers but remaining calm. The crowd that followed her down the Strand were disappointed at Mrs Nation's restraint. The truth was that she was getting old. Four years later, in 1911, she died.

The area between Postoffice and Market Streets was a centre of prostitution from the late 1860s to the 1950s.

In the early days, besides the traditional service, there were 'variety shows' where naked women struck artistic attitudes. One of these shows was interrupted, in 1875, by the sudden onstage appearance of a four-foot alligator. By some accounts the alligator was released by a prankster; others say it emerged from a drain beneath the brothel.

In 1887, the police arrested twenty-seven women of 'disreputable character'. The district really came to the fore around the turn of the century when the harbour was deepened. Then there were more sailors in town than ever before and Galveston became well-known for its red-light district. In 1905 there were complaints about lewd Jewish prostitutes on 28th and Church Street. Some of the brothels offered a discount to medical students.

The two-storey houses had blistered and decrepit exteriors but inside they were comfortably appointed with sofas, subdued lighting and gramophones. The bedrooms were upstairs. The whole area smelt of patchouli.

During the Second World War, a German U-boat came ashore at the western end of the island, so that the crew could enjoy Galveston's famous hospitality. The sailors were satisfied and the U-boat slipped peacefully back into the sea.

The police were only concerned that black customers should keep away from white prostitutes. There were many black prostitutes.

To a great extent, vice was tolerated, even encouraged, but there were limits – homosexuality was insufferable. Any establishment where homosexuals were known to congregate could expect police persecution.

□ □

The Strand Historic District has been painstakingly preserved but it seemed curiously unreal, like a film set or a theme park. Again there were very few people about. The façades of the old buildings were preserved but the interiors had been converted into shopping malls. Inside the malls there were more people, probably employees. There was a shop that sold hats and another that sold frozen yoghurt and a remainder bookshop and a boutique that sold Rastafarian-inspired beachwear to middle-class white people. There was Colonel Bubby's Emporium (an army-surplus store) and a flea-market.

One of the stands in the flea market sold books and I went over to browse. I didn't find any interesting books but I noticed that there were photograph albums for sale, which seemed novel.

I picked up an album. Every single picture inside was of the same woman, a dark-haired, full-figured woman in her early forties. The photos would have been taken twenty years ago. The woman spent a lot of time in her small fenced garden and on the beach. Sometimes she had a dignified meal sitting at a table in front of a serving hatch; she folded her napkin the way they do in restaurants. I imagined she worked in a big hotel as a senior waitress. She was always on her own, never in a group; her lover or friend, the photographer, was never in the pictures. I guess the album contained 200 photos. I wondered who would buy it.

I was thirsty so I looked for a bar. Most of the bars in the area were over-decorated theme joints ('ale pubs') so I walked eastwards, away from the Historic District, along Mechanic Street. At a crossroads there were several dingier places, the seedy dives I prefer.

I chose the Jack Of Diamonds Lounge. It was very dark inside and smelt of sour milk. A mirror-ball hung from the low ceiling, rotating slowly. There was a beer light with a clock and a flowing stream. A brown cardboard sign warned *NO DRUGS ALOUD ON PREMISES & NO SOLICITING*. The place was empty.

The barmaid was a plump Korean woman called Mia. She was wearing a short nightdress of red silk and funny little slippers with pink pompoms. If she had not been wearing make-up I would have assumed she had just got up. She poured my beer, then asked me to buy her a glass of white wine. She kept yawning.

Mia came around to the front of the bar and sat beside me, so close that I could smell her breath when she yawned. 'You come in on ship?'

I told her I hadn't. A long silence. Mia was staring at me, waiting for me to speak. I tried, 'It's quiet in Galveston.'

'Ah, quiet. Is too hot.' She yawned and laid her head on the bar.

The beer tasted faintly of soap.

Mia asked how long I was in town.

Before I could reply, a large and alarming drunk swung through the door, shouting, 'Hellfire! Gimme a goddamn Miller, bitch!' He was red-bearded, like an Irish giant. Mia spoke firmly. 'Get out, you. You eighty-sixed.'

The drunk protested a little, then went outside again.

'He's no problem,' she told me, 'just make a lot of noise. He's my ex-husband, matter of fact. I get you another beer?'

We were joined by a middle-aged man with a sandy moustache, dressed in full camouflage. I asked if he was in the army.

He turned crisply at the waist, looked at me and blew through his nostrils. 'Hardly! These are practically all Russian! The pants are from Argentina! The boots are Timberland!' The snappy man ran an army-surplus store in Houston. He had come down to Colonel Bubby's for a meeting.

I asked him if he always wore army clothing at work. He told me that he wore it all the time. 'It tends to be designed for optimum efficiency, you just can't beat it. Weekends I get to visit with my kids; we like to rough-house in the woods. I got uniforms for them as well; from Singapore – they're kinda undersized. It makes it real fun when we interact.'

There was a second-hand bookshop on 23rd Street; a black schipperke was sleeping in the window. When I walked by, the dog stood up and barked.

Near the bookshop was an intriguing *Santería* shop, selling candles and religious images, amongst a muddle of other sinister curiosities. I wanted to go in but it was closed.

On the same stretch there was an old-fashioned drugstore. Only the soda-fountain was still in use, serving sandwiches and milk shakes. The rest was a threadbare museum; a cabinet of toys from the 1950s, a collection of baggage labels, someone's idea of a *Wunderkammer*.

A Syrian Christian from Kerala, Ray Koshy, had made a 'straw art' exhibition in the old storage gallery. He gathered rice straw of varying shades, which he trimmed into the narrowest strips, then glued onto black paper to build chiaroscuro portraits of television celebrities. It was clear that Mr Koshy was a fine craftsman but his meticulous work, the folk art of a dignified culture, was debased by subjects like Burt Reynolds and Vanna White.

I went into a 7–11 to buy a newspaper. I was the only customer. The middle-aged assistant was bored and restless. His name was Ross and he had recently stopped drinking; he was eager to talk about 'recovery'.

He appeared to have lost some weight at the same time – his clothes looked too big for him. He was like a little bird, or a pullet in a poultry run, the way he moved his neck when he spoke, and the strut of puny defiance. The patches of hair on his head were fair and downy, and he was crimson from the sun. 'You got a car?' he asked. I hadn't, because the island seemed too small for me to need one.

'Hey, I got a Pontiac you can have for seven hundred dollars.'

That was more than I could afford. I was considering buying a bicycle. Ross had one for sale as well. He slapped the counter. 'Fifty bucks.'

He was getting rid of inessentials. It was part of his recovery to trim away the clutter. Also he needed money. He was not ashamed to admit he needed money, he was being honest. He lived in an apartment complex across the road from the 7–11. 'Stay five minutes, then the shifts change and I'll go fetch the bike.'

Early in the evening I bicycled along the sea-wall to a restaurant, where I ordered peppered shrimp. They were served with sourdough bread. I sat outside watching the sun go down. There is a style of restaurant cooking that might be called Gulf Coast Italian (it is very apparent in New Orleans) since it resembles Neapolitan and Sicilian food but has adopted local ingredients such as crawfish and *jalapeños* and avocados; it is not very assertive of its own ethnicity and many a Gulf Coast Italian restaurant describes itself casually as Cajun; indeed a seafood gumbo might appear on the menu, but in reality this is a *zuppa di pesce* with a handful of chopped okra.

Lebanese restaurants will sometimes perform a similar masquerade in Texas: I have entered what appeared to be a Tex-Mex establishment, to discover *falafel* and *ful midames* listed among the *burritos* and *chiles rellenos*.

I was finishing my meal when a man at the next table spoke to me. 'Sir, have you ever considered the end-time?'

He was overweight, wearing a white nylon shirt with damp yellow patches at the armpits and a black tie. His hair was a very short crew cut; it was difficult to identify its colour. He was, I would guess, in his early thirties. Everything suggested religious zeal, so I was wary. I am always being approached by fanatics. Perhaps I shine as a lost soul.

'No,' I replied hesitantly, 'I have never considered the end-time.'

'Do you know about the cobalt bomb?' He rolled a toothpick between finger and thumb.

'No. What is it?'

'The cobalt bomb is the most lethal weapon known to man. It

is made by placing a shield of cobalt-59 metal around a hydrogen bomb. What does that achieve? you may ask. I assure you, sir, that the destructive capacity of the hydrogen bomb is more than doubled by the cobalt-59 casing. But what counts is the hugely increased radioactive contamination. Experts call it the Dirty Bomb. Do you know the Book of Revelations?'

'I've looked at it.'

'Revelations, chapter six, verse twelve. "And I beheld when he had opened the sixth seal, and, lo, there was a great earthquake; and the sun became black as sackcloth of hair, and the moon became as blood." Are you ready for that day?' He jabbed at his back teeth with the wooden pick.

'I shouldn't think there'll be much that I can do about it.'

'Brother,' rejoined the fat man earnestly, putting down the toothpick, 'there is. Do you know of the Rapture?'

'Look. To be honest, I'm not very interested.'

'Where are you from, sir?' asked the fat man.

'England.' I got up to leave.

'Ha. A member of the Common Market! From where the Antichrist shall rise! Nero Caesar shall be reborn!' He had gone quite purple.

The last outburst made me wonder if the fat man was more paranoid than anything else, but later a friend in Houston (who watches Born-Again Christians with horror and fascination) informed me that a fear of the Common Market is in the mainstream of apocalyptic belief. So is a fear of bar-codes.

Four

CAPTAIN GUIDRY, MARY ALICE'S SUGARMAN OF THE MOMENT, WAS making a rare visit to Bolivar. He did not look much like a sea captain to me – I had been expecting a gnarled weather-beaten figure – he looked very unweathered. He was stocky and glistening with sweat; he had the soft ageless quality that I associate with hotel chefs; the result of working indoors over steaming pots. Captain Guidry spoke with a strong Cajun accent. He wore a Miller Lite gimmy-cap and a damp grey T-shirt and beige polyester slacks with a little strap and buckle on both sides of the waistband.

He sat with Mary Alice on the deck, biting his nails. Sweet William had to be shut indoors because Captain Guidry was allergic to his fur. The captain had brought two six-packs of Michelob and a quart of Dr Pepper with him.

I asked Captain Guidry if he had come across Sterling Morrison, who had once played with the Velvet Underground and who now skippers a tugboat on the Intracoastal Waterway. Captain Guidry nodded. 'Sure, I know *Stairling*. He gone to Europe for the summer.'

It was a hot close morning, and the sky was grey and bruisy, trying to rain.

Lucilla brought over a bowl of cheese-and-tomato dip and a huge bag of tortilla chips. Captain Guidry was not allowed to eat cheese.

'Captain, honey, this is Velveeta; it can't hurt you,' Lucilla insisted.

'I wish I could eat it, Lucilla *chère*, but I got the irritable bowel,' he explained.

'I hate him to suffer,' Mary Alice told Lucilla.

'Catfish should be here,' said Lucilla.

'I thought he was goin' overseas, ' said Mary Alice.

'That ain't what I heard. He's been in Morgan City. '

'Is that right? Well, he should be here. With his father dyin'.'

'They got in last night. Catfish *and* Lucan,' announced Sparling, coming out of the house; he had been in the bathroom.

Catfish and Lucan were cousins. Catfish was the son of Cocker-doody and the father of Happy Jack. Lucan had been raised by his uncle, so they were more like brothers than cousins.

Both men had served in the Marine Corps during the Vietnam War. On his second tour Catfish had lost the toes of his right foot. They had both worked on shrimp boats and in the oilfields. Catfish was a diver, working the offshore rigs. Lucan had saved his money and diversified – now he was in the leisure industry with two 'titty bars' in Sulphur, Louisiana. Both rode with the Bandidos though neither had arrived on motorcycles.

Sweet William shot through the door like an eel and jumped onto Mary Alice's lap. 'Baby, baby, you supposed to stay away from Captain Guidry. Now git.' The Italian greyhound slunk away but the captain looked very distressed.

'Lucan too? Oo whee!' Lucilla twisted the top off the Dr Pepper bottle and poured some into a big Dallas Cowboys beaker. 'Reckon it's five years since old Lucan been down here.'

'All of five years,' estimated Mary Alice.

'I just hope those boys gone behave themselves,' muttered Captain Guidry, chewing a hangnail. 'Poo yee.' (That is the Cajun version of 'oo whee'.)

Sparling was horrified that I had bought a bicycle. To him it was a false economy. 'Look at it this way, you movin' on to New Orleans, ain't it? So what you gone do? Ride a pushbike all the way? Man, you should buy a truck. Drive to New Orleans and sell it when you get there. Now you gotta buy a plane ticket – how much that gone cost? How you know you can get rid of that pushbike?'

'I can't afford a truck. Think of the insurance.'

Sparling clicked his tongue dismissively. 'I coulda gotten you a deal.'

'And it doesn't *really* matter if I can't sell the bike when I leave, whereas not being able to sell the truck would be catastrophic.'

His real objection seemed to be that the bicycle was an unmanly form of transport. 'Heck, bubba, nobody rides a pushbike in Bolivar. Only little, little kids. People gone think you a damn weirdo.'

Lucilla had just spent four days with her sister in Slidell, Louisiana, which is very close to New Orleans. She had gone into the city twice while she was there. At the French Market there is a stall that specializes in hot pepper sauces.

'Are they graded by heat?' I asked.

Lucilla had brought home a generous selection. 'The hottest one is called Religious Experience.'

She told us she had almost had a genuine religious experience. Along from the pepper-sauce stall, at the far end of the market, where Decatur joins Esplanade, there was a stall, selling incense and crystals and African-style jewellery, run by a thin black woman all dressed in purple robes. Lucilla complimented the woman on her outfit.

The woman was a member of the Nahziryah Monastic Community,

the Order of the Purple Veil, and she had presented Lucilla with a booklet entitled *The Purple Veil.* The order's symbol was a Star of David (above a sickle moon) emanating rays of light. Its founder was the Nazir Moreh K. B. Kedem, a black man with knee-length purple dreadlocks, purple robes and dangling purple crystal earrings.

Lucilla showed us the booklet. 'It's kinda beautiful. Listen.' The excerpts she read were much as one would expect:

> Those who follow the spiritual path enter into one of the seven rays which lead to immortality; while those who do follow the material path enter the ray that leads to ultimate crystallization. Both lead to darkness – one to the immortal darkness of divine union, and the other to the mortal darkness of divine annihilation.
>
> I come to you, open your heart that I might get thru to you . . .
> Do nothing that will stop me from getting thru . . .
> I will sing to you in your dreams –
> I will come to you when your heart screams
> of those things that will bring you pain,
> all the shame . . .
> Even if you are to blame,
> I will ease your pain . . .
> If you call on Me . . . try to open your eyes to see . . .
> Oh hear those things that come from Me –
> your eyes will see –
> you will walk with me throughout eternity . . .

Mary Alice sighed. 'That is so *special.* I just gotta read that book.'

Lucilla sighed too, folding her hands in her lap. 'You know, there is just so much wisdom to be found in unexpected places.' She gave me a meaningful glance.

Mary Alice asked if I could do calligraphy. She wanted me to copy out the Nazir's words so that she could frame them. 'Maybe you could do it on parchment. Can y'all buy parchment still? That would be real neat.'

It struck me that anybody could start a cult, with the right outfit and the right language.

On the subject of books Mary Alice proceeded to tell me, in some detail, the plot of a novel she had read called *The Storm-Tossed Crown* by Genivere Crawley Flaxman. It was her favourite book. It was about the Queen of England – but there was some confusion as to which one. I tried to help. 'Was it about Queen Elizabeth or Mary, Queen of Scots? Queen Victoria?'

'No, honey, I don't think so. Let me think. Was there a Queen Samantha?'

Queen Samantha travelled about her kingdom in a silver carriage and she had many lovers: one was a knight in armour, another had explored Africa.

'Y'all understand, she was a real strong woman and if she wanted some lovin' she just went for it, but her advisers tried to stop her, sayin' it wasn't becomin' to a queen to carry on like that, all of them turned against her, that is except for the palace monk, he was on her side and, well, it turned out that he was really her brother and he was supposed to be the king himself . . .'

Mary Alice must have noticed my eyes glazing because she interrupted herself. 'Well, I guess I won't tell you the whole story. Y'all just look out for that one, honey. *The Storm-Tossed Crown* by Genivere Crawley Flaxman.'

I looked over the railing and saw an old man wheeling a supermarket trolley full of empty cans along the road. The old man had a clear plastic tube running from his left nostril into a hole bored through his left cheek.

□ □

Catfish was tall and ruddy, covered with indistinct blue tattoos, and had ginger hair, a flowing beard; he looked like a Viking. Muscles twisted about his red arms in serpentine coils, as if they had attached themselves from elsewhere, like vines. He shuffled up to the House of Blue Lights at noon, with a flagon of Wild Turkey and a bag of ice. He was wearing a black T-shirt with a map of Vietnam and the legend *When I Die I'll Go To Heaven*

Cause I've Done My Time In Hell.

Lucilla whooped like a cowgirl when she saw him. 'Yee ha! You come right on up here, you old firecracker!'

The women hugged Catfish, squealing like two happy jackals. Sparling slapped him on the back, wagging his cigarette up and down with his teeth in a comic gesture of pleasure.

Mary Alice introduced me. Catfish's hand had the texture of pumice.

She asked if he remembered Captain Guidry. Catfish shook his hand as well. 'How y'all doin, brother?' The captain muttered a reply, somewhat warily.

There was a frantic scratching at the screen door. 'Sweet William, son of a gun!' exclaimed Catfish, releasing the dog, who leapt straight into his arms to lick his face.

Mary Alice touched Captain Guidry's knee. 'Baby, please. Sweet William's just crazy about Catfish.'

Whisky was splashed into plastic beakers. Catfish smiled lazily. 'Ain't no place like home,' he said, and closed his eyes.

'I guess he must be tired,' whispered Mary Alice maternally.

I asked Lucilla why he was called Catfish; he didn't look much like one.

Lucilla smiled. 'Well, I guess that's true but he was real slippery as a young 'un.'

Two hours later Lucan drove up in a white Dodge truck, with an upright object in the back covered by a tarpaulin. Princess sat beside him, talking excitedly.

Lucan was shorter than Catfish, dark and clean-shaven, with a baggy face, like a younger Walter Matthau. He wore a straw cowboy hat, which he removed as he approached the house, and a white T-shirt with a Lone Star flag and *Don't Mess With Texas* on it.

Princess raced up the steps ahead of him; if you unfocused your eyes she was running upstairs with a beachball in her arms. She had a wild look, flashing green eyes. 'You all got any liquor? I need somethin' to smooth out the edges.'

'Why, Lucan Courbet! Still as fine-lookin' as ever!' Mary Alice called out.

'Ain't you just! Oo whee!' shrieked Lucilla.

Catfish had fallen asleep on a sun-lounger, Sweet William pressed to his side. He was snoring loudly.

Sparling was getting drunk; he was telling Captain Guidry how much he loved Ronny Sue, that nobody was going to take her from him.

Captain Guidry, who had had very little to drink all day, looked anxious and bored; clearly his intention had been to be alone with Mary Alice. Sparling kept exhaling menthol cigarette smoke all over him, which he would swish away disapprovingly.

Princess filled a glass with ice and whisky, then announced that she had taken Methedrine.

Lucilla shook her head sadly. 'That little baby of yours gone be a party animal.'

Lucan patted Mary Alice's bottom affectionately. 'Got a present for you, girl, down there on the truck.'

'Oh, that looks like a piano. You know I can't play no piano.'

'It ain't a piano,' said Lucan, 'but you 'long the right lines.'

'It's a jukebox,' Princess revealed, spoiling the surprise.

'Y'all kiddin' me?' asked Mary Alice.

'No shit,' said Princess, 'I seen it already.'

'Yup. I picked it up in Vinton. Fella there owed me a little money from a card game. He was kinda disinclined to pay up. Figured you could use some music round the house.'

Lucan, Sparling and I went down to unload the jukebox. Captain Guidry stayed on the deck because he had a slipped disc that prevented him from bending and lifting.

It was a 1970s Rock-O-La, cumbersome and heavier than one would have thought. When we got the jukebox inside, and it was plugged in, Lucilla sighed. 'Now you can bet none of us got any quarters.'

'No problem. I fixed it so's it don't need money. Just go ahead and play the damn thing.'

The selections, on hand-written cards, had a marked regional flavour. There was Barbara Lynn's 'You'll Lose A Good Thing', Tommy McLain's 'Sweet Dreams', Slim Harpo's 'Rainin' In My Heart', Freddy Fender's 'Wasted Days And Wasted Nights', Johnny Paycheck's 'Take This Job And Shove It', Marty Robbins' 'El Paso' and 'All Around Cowboy'; there were many country-and-western songs by singers I had never heard of, and there was Delbert McClinton singing Otis Redding's tragic ballad 'I've Got Dreams To Remember', and Jerry Lee Lewis singing 'Look Me Up On Your Way Down'; 'Breakin' Up Is Hard To Do' by Jivin' Gene and 'Mathilda' by Cookie and the Cupcakes.

Apart from country-and-western, soul and dance tunes, there was plenty of the slow 1950s-style rock and roll that has never gone out of fashion in this part of America. Some critics, recognizing the tendency, call the music Swamp Pop; the strongest influence is Fats Domino and the performers may be black or white.

Only one song on the jukebox could be classified as purely Cajun (as opposed to Swamp Pop) and that was 'Jole Blon' by the fiddler Harry Choates. It has a haunting, almost keening lyric – sung by Choates in barely comprehensible French – that is offset powerfully by the arrangement, which isn't doleful at all but jaunty, swinging in a sexy relaxed way, as if urging the listener to forget the pains of rejection, find someone else and dance.

'Jole Blon' was a hit in 1946 and it was certainly the first Cajun record to cross over into the wider general field of country music. Even today, nearly half a century later, it retains its appeal and you can find it on jukeboxes across Louisiana and Texas.

Harry Choates is an interesting and tragic figure. There is a stereotype, in most forms of popular music, of the self-destructive genius: Robert Johnson, Charlie Parker, Hank Williams, Jimi Hendrix, pioneers who widen the possibilities of the music but burn out in the process. Harry Choates died in a jail cell in Austin when he was only twenty-eight years old.

He was born in Rayne, Louisiana, in December 1922. His father seems to have abandoned his mother, Tave Manard Choates, who took the boy with her across the Sabine River to Port Arthur, Texas, in 1929 or 1930.

Harry Choates never went to school and spoke English as a second language. As a child he learnt to play the fiddle and the guitar. Legend has it that he could play from the first time he handled a fiddle and, strangely, Harry Choates never owned a musical instrument; even at the height of his fame he played a borrowed fiddle.

Port Arthur was a tough place; the boy's playgrounds were honky-tonks and dance-halls, and he was an alcoholic from the age of twelve. He made a living playing in barber shops, where customers would throw coins to the urchin. By his late teens Choates was playing with dance bands such as Leo Soileau's Cajun Aces.

Port Arthur was, and still is, a centre of Cajun culture outside Louisiana. Any touring band from Port Arthur could therefore play two overlapping circuits; they could go eastwards to perform at the Cajun dance-halls of southwestern Louisiana, but they could also go west into Texas proper, to take what had been a purely regional folk music to a larger non-Cajun audience.

This broadening of the music's appeal meant that it had to be modified but not diluted. Harry Choates, more than any other Cajun musician, understood this demand; into songs that remained steadfastly Cajun he worked elements of jazz and blues and the honky-tonk country music of the oilfields. Specifically he was influenced by another hybrid music, Western Swing. Western Swing bands brought improvization and jazz aesthetics to traditional mountain tunes, a fusion that produced a new vibrant dance music at once familiar and innovative. Choates similarly transformed Cajun music and he took the dance-halls by storm.

When the Second World War started, Harry Choates enlisted in the army but he was quickly discharged for drunkenness. He went to work in a shipyard in Orange, just north of Port Arthur.

At night and at weekends he played his music with a variety of bands. There were more dates than ever because of the new army camps and air bases along the Gulf Coast. Choates became more and more flamboyant, dancing about the stage as he played and sang, the music becoming looser and wilder, and his drinking got more out of hand.

A publicity shot from 1945 shows him standing at the microphone, a skinny youth wearing a suit and a dark bow-tie, playing the fiddle with his head thrown back and his mouth wide open as if he is laughing or shouting.

In the same year he married Helen Daenen, who knew all about his drinking. A photograph shows Harry slumped against her, his right arm about her neck; he looks like Billy the Kid but very tired. Helen beams nervously at the camera; she is as delicate as a little bird. She was convinced that she could mend his ways. The marriage was doomed. In 1946 the Gold Star music company of Houston offered a recording contract.

'Jole Blon' brought Harry Choates instant fame. He toured incessantly, playing joints like Speedy's Broken Mirror in Sulphur and road-houses all along Highway 90.

Sometimes he was too drunk to play; sometimes, when he did play, fights broke out and he would jump from the stage to join in, using his borrowed fiddle as a weapon. He would smash a liquor-store window to get a bottle of whisky and he was often arrested.

In 1950 Helen, who had borne him two children, filed for divorce. The following year Choates was charged with contempt of court in a marital desertion case; he had neglected to pay the $20 weekly maintenance payments. The police placed him in Travis County Jail, Austin, and refused him bail. He was to await trial in Beaumont.

In jail Harry Choates apparently went into violent delirium tremens, pounding his head against the bars (others claim the wardens beat him) until his skull was shattered. He died on 17 July 1951.

His grave in Port Arthur is inscribed *Parrain De La Musique Cajun.*

Lucilla played the first song, 'Tequila', by The Champs. Mary

Alice giggled and started to perform a 1960s go-go dance, a dance that would have a name like The Frug. Lucilla joined in.

'Way to go!' yelled Sparling, excited in some deep, quick part of his mind by the sight of two women dancing.

Catfish woke up, opened a Michelob, drank it, then stood up slowly, a little unsteadily, but smiling at the unsteadiness.

Lucan stood with his arm around Princess. Captain Guidry looked fed up.

The next song was 'Walk Through This World With Me' by George Jones. Catfish, with the same sleepy smile, put his arms around Mary Alice, as placidly as rolling over in bed, and they danced very slowly.

Lucan held his arms out in exactly the position for Lucilla to drop effortlessly into them.

I tried to dance with Princess, with some difficulty because her stomach was so enormous; also she insisted on smoking. We persevered through Rod Bernard's 'This Should Go On Forever'.

If I had to name the most typical example of a Swamp Pop song, it would be 'This Should Go On Forever'. The tune goes around and around like something medieval – and is almost beautiful just because it goes around and around – a drawing of the serpent devouring his own tail.

Sparling swerved over to the jukebox. 'I'm the goddamn DJ, this is Sparling's heartbreak half-hour, y'all.' He chose Dorsey Clanton's 'Black Jack David', a folk-song (that I have known since kindergarten) performed as a gently rocking waltz, with a Cajun fiddle and an accordion to give a Louisiana feel to what must be a Scottish song.

Princess leant forward, closing her eyes; I could see the tiny red and blue veins in her eyelids, which seemed lit from behind by the very brightness of her eyes. She stood on tiptoe to rest her chin on my shoulder and her teeth were rattling from the Methedrine.

'Black Jack David came ridin' through the woods,
Singing so loud and merry.
His voice rang out through the green, green trees
And he charmed the heart of a maiden.
He charmed the heart of a maiden.'

'Why, this is such a sad old song,' whispered Mary Alice.
'Guess that old boy's feelin' blue,' said Catfish.

'Listen to me, lass. My name is Jack,
I've wandered far and wide.
Lookin' for a fair-haired lass like you;
Won't you come and be my bride?
Come and be my bride.'

Sparling was singing along, but his voice was too exaggerated to harmonize, looping upwards, looser than the tight structure of the melody. Lucilla laughed and complained that he sounded like an old hound dog. Princess's jaw continued to vibrate on my shoulder.

'Yes, I'll forsake my husband dear,
I'll even forsake my baby.
I'll forsake my fine, fine home
To go with you, Black Jack David.
To go with you, Black Jack David.

Last night she slept on a four-poster bed
Beside her husband and baby
But tonight she'll sleep on the cold, cold ground
Beside her Black Jack David.
Beside her Black Jack David.'

When the song ended, there was a pause while we waited for the next one. 'Black Jack David' started all over again. 'Oh, Sparling, it was fine once, honey.' It came on a third time and we stopped dancing. Sparling's heartbreak half-hour consisted of the one song played eight or nine times.

In Princess's teenage world formalities were observed, and that there had been dancing made the occasion a dance; I was her partner and therefore the focus of her attention for the rest of the afternoon. 'You ever look at old Serena Sabak?' she asked me.

Serena Sabak (America's Sexiest Psychic) gives advice to readers of the *Weekly World News*. Her address is a post-office box in Dallas. In the byline photograph she has a blond mane, one hoop earring, a double string of pearls and a ring on every finger of both hands. She is making an intense but amiable face: leaning forward and peering with inquisitive black eyes. She does not, to be honest, look particularly sexy; she looks like an alert little dog. Both hands are rubbing a crystal ball.

Princess had written to Serena Sabak early in her pregnancy, asking if she was bearing the reincarnation of Jimi Hendrix, but Serena Sabak had not answered her enquiry. Princess remained a fan, however, and the *Weekly World News* was the only newspaper she ever read.

She had the latest issue in the truck and she went down to get it for me. 'Now you all read this,' she urged me.

> Dear Serena: I have a strange problem that has me baffled. I woke up yesterday with a big tattoo of a woman on my left arm. I don't have any idea how it got there and I hadn't even been outside my house the night before it appeared. I'm afraid no-one will believe me when I tell them it just appeared out of nowhere. You're the only person who can help me figure out where it came from and how I can get rid of it. Does it mean I was a sailor in a former life? – Puzzled in Sherburne.

> Dear Puzzled: The tattoo on your arm is of your great-great-grandmother, who died 30 years before you were born. Her spirit has been watching over you for 18 years and she has decided to let you see what she looks like. Take a photo of the tattoo – because it will disappear within a few days and will

never appear again.

I told Princess that I had read an article in the *National Enquirer* about a baby born with fillings and a gold tooth, taken to be proof of reincarnation.

Lucilla scolded me: 'Joseph, that is so tactless.'

Mary Alice was disdainful of such papers. 'Y'all read about Elvis runnin' about in some shoppin' mall, or livin' with some old girl he wouldn't have looked at! Just the most wicked lies.'

It started to rain heavily. Captain Guidry bustled downstairs to roll up his windows. His car was, to his horror, full of cats. When he came back up he remarked, 'Quite a wind fixin' out there; could cut up rough.'

By late evening all the visitors had gone home. It was still raining but the wind had weakened. There would not be a hurricane.

I remembered Nadia's account of the waters rolling over La Marque and boats passing along Highway 3. When the flood subsided, an angry water-moccasin was stranded in their kitchen. Misia had stunned it with a frying-pan. I could picture Misia swinging the frying-pan as an ancient Muscovite cudgel. Nadia called a neighbour, who dragged the senseless snake onto the front lawn with a spade, then shot it through the head.

Why did he bother to shoot it? I had asked her; if the water-moccasin was knocked out, he could have decapitated it with the side of the spade. Nadia explained that the neighbour was a member of the National Rifle Association.

Mary Alice told me about a tornado that went through Buna when she was thirteen. All the children were kept inside the school and told to stay away from the windows. But the temptation to watch the devastation constantly got the better of them. Along the main street a derelict house was gradually dismantled by the wind; first the roof, then the windows, as if the wind had a childish curiosity about the building.

Several parked cars and trucks were blown over. A very old dog had been cowering in the back of one of the fallen trucks; it was a black mongrel bitch that belonged to Hal Pennet, a mechanic.

Mary Alice, the friend of all animals, knew Pennet's bitch and burst into frightened tears when she saw her staggering in confusion, trying to stand up to the wind. She begged the teacher to let her bring the dog indoors. The teacher forbade her but she ran to the door.

Outside, the wind, that had been mainly a visual phenomenon, rushed through Buna like a great train made of glass. Mary Alice's feet were pushed from beneath her and for a moment she was aboard the glass train, flying sideways down Main Street.

She clung to a traffic sign and watched the front wall peel off the derelict house, catching the old dog as it split into planks, killing her outright.

As Mary Alice told me this, she hugged Sweet William to her bosom, and I think he understood the emotion in the story because he tipped his head back to nuzzle her ear.

§

Galveston's residents were familiar with hurricanes, indeed they had dogged the history of the settlement. Lafitte's stronghold had been flattened by the 1818 storm. In 1837 a storm had blown down a custom-house that had only been operating for two days. An Episcopal church had crashed down in 1842. The Strand was flooded in 1854 and a steamer snapped in two. The docks were destroyed in the terrible storm of 1867 when four ships, with their anchors dragging, were blown across the railway bridge. But by the end of the century an air of confidence rested over the city. The ground floors of dwellings and offices were raised several feet, as a safeguard against what were referred to as 'overflows' – in other words, occasions for merriment: half-days for clerks, and children splashing in the street. On Tuesday, 4 September 1900, the Washington office of the Weather Bureau cabled the

Galveston office: TROPICAL STORM DISTURBANCE MOVING NORTHWARD OVER CUBA.

By Thursday the storm's centre was nearer the mainland, veering in from just northwest of the Florida Keys. By Friday morning the storm's centre was moving parallel to the Louisiana coast, and the Galveston Weather Bureau was warned of the increasing likelihood of a hurricane.

The weatherman Joseph Cline routinely ran two pennants from the flagpole on top of the Levy Building. Nobody was unduly alarmed by the warning, for the working week was nearly over and, although the skies had looked threatening earlier in the evening, by midnight they seemed to have calmed down, and no further telegraphs arrived from the Washington Bureau.

There was, however, the quietest wind and the weatherman Cline noticed that long swells were breaking on the shore, and that the tide was higher than average. He woke up at four to find that the sea had become turbulent and was still rising. At five he cabled the Washington office:

> UNUSUALLY HEAVY SWELLS FROM THE SOUTHEAST, INTERVALS ONE TO FIVE MINUTES, OVERFLOWING LOW PLACES SOUTH PORTION OF CITY THREE TO FOUR BLOCKS FROM BEACH. SUCH HIGH WATER WITH OPPOSING WIND NEVER OBSERVED PREVIOUSLY.

Cline rode up and down the beach warning the citizens to shelter, but few seemed concerned. By seven, spectators thronged the promenade to enjoy the great brown waves raging at the shoreline. Beach huts and a couple of small piers were chewed up before an appreciative crowd.

The film director King Vidor was a boy of six at the time; he remembered watching the waves with his mother, and feeling that they were inside 'a bowl looking up toward the level of the sea. I felt as if the sea was going to break over the edge of the bowl and come pouring down upon us,' and very soon the sea did, flooding the streets in the lower areas of the city. It suddenly got very cold, and a skiffing wind drove the spectators back indoors.

•

At ten o'clock Cline received a telegraph from Washington indicating that the storm was changing direction, from northwest to northeast. He ran up a pennant accordingly. It was immediately shredded by the wind. Moments later the flagpole was snapped off. Cline recognized that the island was in the blades of a vortex.

By noon the two causeways that linked the island to the mainland were submerged. The wooden pavement blocks of the business area were floating about in muddy water. At half past two all the telegraph wires were down. Bricks, lumber, slates and glass swept through the air. The last recorded wind speed was 84 miles per hour, before the wind-gauge on top of the Levy building shattered. Cline estimated that the winds reached over 110, maybe even 120, miles per hour.

At six o'clock the bell of St Mary's Cathedral sounded the Angelus; the tower swayed, and there was a silence that cut straight across a toll, for the great two-ton bell had been ripped from its iron bands.

Wooden houses were shattered. Brick buildings were flattened by the undermining waves. Debris in the streets formed dams that caused the flooding of even the highest raised houses. Fifteen feet of water covered the city.

People clung to their roofs, only to find the houses collapsing beneath them. An iron streetcar trestle, with its ties, crosspieces and rails, became a 200-foot spinning battering ram.

About a thousand people took refuge in the Ursuline Convent. When the north wall of the convent collapsed, a group of black citizens started to wail hymns but were silenced by the mother superior, who allowed only silent prayer.

A woman gave birth in a nun's cell.

All over the city there were frantic baptisms; sinners, assured of death, sought redemption. All night long the sea churned the city around and around, and over six thousand people were drowned before the waters rolled away.

On Sunday morning there was a clear bright sky, and a sea that was quiet, as if weakened by its outburst. A photograph shows a great field of planks and furniture, shutters and poles – 1,500 acres of devastation.

Three thousand six hundred homes had been destroyed. The pumping-station had disappeared, as had the streetcar and the railway station, along with the trains. There were no telegraph or telephone lines.

A 4000-ton British ship, the *Taunton*, had been propelled twenty-two miles from high water, ploughing a groove through the sodden coastland. Another British steamer, the *Roma*, had careered sideways down the ship channel, knocking away three bridges. The lightship, moored between the jetties by a 1,500-lb anchor and sixty fathoms of chain, was discovered four miles across the bay.

The bodies of humans and animals, bloated and softened by the salt water, began to smell in the late summer heat.

The mayor of Galveston, Walter C. Jones, formed the Central Relief Committee; the citizens worked efficiently at restoring some degree of order; trapped survivors were rescued, the injured cared for.

Six volunteers sailed a yacht across the bay towards Texas City; they found that the storm had flooded inland for some ten miles, and they were crossing a waterlogged prairie that was dotted with carrion, until they came across a railway line, and, a mile further on, a handcar, and they pumped fifteen miles before meeting a train bound for Houston.

The authorities there responded quickly; a relief party of 250 men arrived in Galveston on Monday morning.

Meanwhile the burial squad worked as methodically as possible but, though formal inquests were waived and little attempt was made at investigation, the magnitude of the task soon proved daunting. The ground was too wet to dig mass graves. It became a question of gathering the corpses to one central location. The crews worked with camphor-soaked handkerchiefs over their noses, and were given rations of whisky.

So many bodies were hauled from the rubble that it was decided to dump the dead out at sea. Funeral boats chugged eighteen miles into the Gulf; the bodies were weighted with rocks and dropped overboard. The next day, however, several of the bodies washed up on West Beach. Thereafter relief workers were instructed to burn corpses upon discovery.

For nearly two months there were pungent bonfires, and people on the mainland observed the yellow light of the pyres. By Christmas any corpse found was a skeleton. The last – that of a teenage girl – was found on 10 February.

Looting broke out but reports vary as to the extent: the national press claimed that seventy-five looters were shot by armed vigilantes; the *Galveston Daily News* reported only eight: all black men, so perhaps it was a case of not wishing to shame the relatives of the white looters. Looters were discouraged by the introduction of a pass system to travel on and off the island, and the declaration of martial law: by Thursday the 13th there were some 2,000 armed police and militia on the island.

Nearly two months after the storm forty-five cadavers were discovered in a swamp, all with their pockets turned out.

Bolivar, much less populated, had also suffered, though 125 people had huddled inside the lighthouse and were saved. Three entire families, their staff and their beasts, disappeared at Rollover Pass; an accurate death toll has never been recorded but between 50 and 100 seems likely. Water supplies became contaminated by decaying cadavers, forcing all survivors temporarily to abandon the peninsula.

The city of Galveston recovered from the storm with extraordinary speed. Within a week the telegraph and water supply were restored. Within a fortnight workmen had cleared most of the rubble; underground telephone lines were laid and the railway bridge was rebuilt. On 22 September martial law was revoked. The harbour was back in action and the electric trolley ran again. Construction began on a raised sea-wall to prevent further disasters.

For some years afterwards one of the most popular spectacles at Coney Island's Dreamland was a mechanical re-enactment of the Great Galveston Flood of 1900. Galveston was associated in the public mind with hurricanes. That was bad for the port's reputation.

The Houston Ship Canal was created and Houston took over as the port of Texas. The Galveston docks stayed in operation: bananas and peanuts passed through but not the more lucrative petroleum.

Now containers are loaded and unloaded at Galveston. The docks are full of cranes lifting giant nursery blocks, in candy colours; there could be anything inside the containers. A large area of dockland has been given over to tourism; there is a tall ship, the *Elissa*, a restaurant called Willie G's, and a museum.

Hurricanes, of course, continued to attack; the most violent was that of 1915, which killed 275 people in the vicinity. At High Island there stands a cedar tree renowned for its part in local history: nine people were saved by climbing into its branches.

There were hurricanes in 1932, 1938, 1940, 1941, 1942, 1943 and 1947. In 1949 a hurricane with a wind speed of 135 miles an hour was recorded.

Hurricanes started to have names, as if they were monsters that had been tamed, existing mainly to be observed by scientists. In 1957 there was Hurricane Audrey; in 1959, Hurricane Debra; in 1961, Hurricane Carla, when wind speeds exceeding 175 miles an hour, killed thirty-four people and injured 475. In 1963 there was Hurricane Cindy. In 1970 there was Hurricane Celia. In 1974 there was Hurricane Carmen. In 1983 Hurricane Alicia killed seventeen Bolivar residents.

Five

THE COFFEE AT PIRATE'S COVE WAS WEAK BUT YOU COULD HAVE AS MANY refills as you wanted. Mr Advani had become very friendly; he liked to talk about his years in Bombay. He had lived in a district called Andheri East and he was thrilled that I had stayed there myself. I said, 'I know who comes from Andheri – Madurai Dixit.' I remembered a newspaper article about the pretty actress. Mr Advani clapped his hands and exclaimed, 'Yes! That is right! Madurai Dixit was born in Andheri. I believe it is where her parents live still.'

Mr Advani drove down to Galveston every day from Clearlake, south of Houston (where NASA is based), crossing to Bolivar on the ferry. He had many relatives in the Houston area. His 85-year-old mother was soon to join him from Baroda.

The motel had eighteen rooms, six of which were occupied by his younger relatives (nephews and cousins). At night they looked after the business and the convenience store rattled to the strains of FM radio; they wore bright printed shirts and were eager to assimilate as quickly as possible.

My having mentioned Madurai Dixit became distorted to my knowing her personally. I was often questioned about other Bombay film stars. 'What about Amitabh – you have met him?'

I rode my bicycle along the hard shoulder of Highway 87 towards the ferry landing. It was a hot morning and the sea gave off an oily, fishy stench. Two men were standing in the water beyond the reeds, dragging a seine. A flattened snake stretched across my path. On the other side of the highway was the lighthouse, 117 feet tall, covered in black steel plates.

Shifting sand-bars and an uneven sea bed had always made Galveston Bay difficult to enter. An earlier lighthouse, built in 1852, had once stood on the site but that one was pulled down in the Civil War; the Confederate commander in Texas decided it would steer enemy ships to the port.

The present lighthouse went up in 1872. It had a 51,000-candle-power revolving light, protected by wire netting, for ducks and geese were inclined to crash into the glass. Two raised cottages stand near its base, where the keepers lived.

One foggy November afternoon in 1917, the lighthouse was attacked by artillery fire for nearly two hours. The people of Bolivar assumed that a German battleship was attacking the town. In fact the aggressors were American troops from Fort San Jacinto who were muddled on exercise by the poor visibility. After the First World War, a system of jetties and buoys was considered a more practical means of guiding ships into the bay and the light was extinguished in 1933.

From what I understood, the peninsula had changed very little over the years. It could have changed beyond recognition, for an attempt was made to turn Port Bolivar into a major port. The Santa Fe Railroad bought out the old Gulf and Interstate Railroad in 1908 and restored the track along the peninsula.

A pier, large enough to berth three ships and costing $300,000, was built at the Fort Travis terminal. In June 1909 the first cargo ship sailed in, bringing 1,000 tons of New England granite for the new federal building in Houston.

In 1912 the Santa Fe experimented with a special iron ore dock, 325 feet long and 58 feet high, that cost $40,000. It was a temporary construction to see if it was worth shipping iron ore (from Ore City in nearby Upshur County) to the industrial Northeast.

In 1913 5,550 tons of iron ore were loaded onto ships at Port Bolivar. Other cargoes included cottonseed cake, steel rails, livestock and salt. Forty-six million feet of lumber were shipped out of the port.

In 1914 hope faded; the outbreak of war in Europe and the German threat to Atlantic shipping made it hard to attract investors; then the 1915 hurricane caused so much damage, washing away miles of track, that the whole venture was considered too hazardous.

I rode past a queue of cars and trucks waiting to board the ferry. When it arrived the attendant would not let me board; he sent me to the back of the queue. Then when we came to disembark at Galveston the same attendant would not let me off until every vehicle had left.

I felt that he was being unreasonable and told him so. I had wheeled the bike onto the ferry before with no interference. I had been able to slip on and off with the pedestrians.

'OK, man, how much tax you pay on that bicycle? This service is paid for by the taxpayers. They pay my wages. I ain't givin' out no privileges to untaxed vehicles – get outta here! What you give me?'

I passed the morning reading and swimming and lying in the sun, just along from Stewart Beach. It was a Friday and there were quite a few people dotted about. A woman played in the waves with a lean fawn dog that I took to be a Saluki (I found out later it was a clipped Afghan hound) and people were boogie-boarding, riding the surf on short polystyrene floats. Every so often I would fall asleep.

A youngish Hispanic man with a dazed raptor look (aquiline, but without precision or focus) approached me. He wanted to know if I was a journalist; he wanted 'access to the media'. When I asked him why, he told me that he had grown up in California where, over a course of five years in the 1970s, he had been sexually abused by Ronald Reagan. It sounded a bit unlikely. If it was true, surely any number of investigative newspapers would jump at the story?

'Nobody believes me, man.'

'There must be some way that you can prove it?'

'It's real hard, man. See, he used to disguise himself as my grandpa. I even thought he was my grandpa at the time. Guess I was deluding myself. But I been in hospital and they give me memory drugs, you see, and now I can tell plainly that it was in fact Ronald Reagan. Just can't get nobody to believe me.' He wandered off to try some other people.

On Tremont Street I watched a middle-aged man scaling the front wall of a wooden apartment house to let himself in through an upstairs window; it was an impressive feat because he was clinging to the slats with his fingertips. He was calm and steady in all his movements, considering he was eighteen feet or more off the ground; then I wondered if he was a cat burglar, in that he must have had some opportunities to develop his extraordinary skill.

Maybe, dazed by the sun, I had watched a criminal at work; then again, maybe he was a circus performer.

§

On 10 September 1932, a flying creature was seen near the City cemetery at 40th and Broadway. Witnesses told police that the creature resembled a skinny middle-aged man in most respects, except that he had large strangely-shaped ears, and eyes, like those of an animal, without whites. Some claimed they saw short black horns on his head. He had been flying around all day, disrupting workplaces, wrecking grocery stores, and hurling abuse at respectable women. The flying was not of the outspread-arms variety; instead he leapt extraordinary distances. With one bound, the creature could jump onto the roof of a single-storey dwelling and he was so sure-footed that he could climb the sides of higher buildings like a Human Fly. The creature was prone to disappear if anybody tried to catch him; once he was collared but he struggled free, giving his would-be captor a very nasty bite. The nuisance became known as the Devil Man.

That evening he harassed a newly-wed couple who refused him a lift in their automobile, running apace with their car for over four miles, pulling faces, until the woman fainted. For days the Devil Man caused mischief, shouting insults from aloft.

The police, who had at first treated the complaints as a joke, even a publicity stunt for a travelling show, started to take the matter seriously. Police Chief Tony Messina organized a party that, by means of poles and nets, captured a wild-eyed, long-haired man from the roof of a grain warehouse. The man's name was Heinrich Schwab.

Schwab told the arresting officers that he came from the hills of Arkansas, where he was a disciple of the 'great spiritual monarch' King Zulu, 'the benefactor and adviser to Neptune', who would only come to those who could speak his language.

'Are you the Devil Man?' asked Chief Messina.

'No, I am greater than the Devil,' replied Schwab.

The proprietor of the Rhineland Inn, a man called George Hartman, came to Schwab's defence, saying that the Devil Man was a harmless lunatic.

'That poor soul came into my place. He told me he was hungry, and said "I'm from the hills of Arkansas. My ears look like they are waiting for to hear the up-yonder spirits and my eyes look like they are looking for the moon. Even the Devil would feed me." I could see the man was hungry, so I gave him a piece of pie, some milk and a sandwich. I'll admit he did look funny. He wanted to get hold of a trumpet. I said: "Save your pennies, hobo." Well, 'long about that time some schoolchildren came along and started laughing at the man, who was standing in front of my place now. They kidded him so much that he became angry, and he said, "If you don't let me alone, I'm goin' to put the Devil on you!" Then the kids started yelling, "Devil Man! Devil Man!" They drew such a crowd that the man got scared and ran off. Then the story got about that he disappeared into the graveyard. Some of the beer parlors began saying that the Devil Man had been to their joints, bought whiskey and disappeared. They said he would come back, and crowds of people would hang around these places in hopes of seeing him, some of them carrying guns and rifles. Of course most of them would buy drinks and plenty of them. One fellow said, "If the Devil Man takes me to Hell I want to be good and drunk." One of the places put a sign outside, saying the Devil Man was doing all his drinking in that bar. And the people went for it. They packed the place.'

Louis Kohlman told the police that the business at Kohlman's Bar had doubled.

Hiram Carp was less enthusiastic about Schwab frequenting his establishment. 'The people wouldn't come out at night, especially when they heard this Devil Man had poured whiskey down a woman's back outside my place.'

On the night of 13 September, though Schwab was safely incarcerated there were five reported sightings of demonic figures in Galveston. A flying man caused havoc in the Garten Verein Pavilion, and another disrupted the second – and final – assembly of the Mystic Order of Apollonians. The police began to wonder if Schwab was their man.

Questioned by excited reporters, Schwab made the following statement:

> 'My name is Heinrich Schwab, and I am the Devil Man – but greater than the Devil. I came from the high black hills of Arkansas on September the 6th, 1932. I walked under the stars and Neptune guided me through the darkness of the night until I reached Port Arthur, Texas, and from there I made my way to Eminence in Liberty County; then I came to Galveston Bay, still under the guidance of Neptune and possibly one of his assistant stars. I came to Galveston as the sun came down in the skies.
>
> 'Yes, they got me in jail, but it's my spirit that is haunting the people, because I have not been treated right by the police. That's why I'm going to keep on troubling them. If I wanted I could get out of sight right now – I could disappear away from all of you . . .'

A policeman interjected that the prisoner had indeed 'disappeared' once from his cell, to be recaptured at Shaughnessy's, a few blocks from the station.

> 'You want to know how I got my powers? Well, Neptune came to me in the form of a fish-hook in June of 1919. I was reading my Bible at the time. Oh, yes, I'm a Lutheran, but I believe in the Divine too. Neptune told me to walk straight ahead, that I would find a two-headed man stranded on a rock. I found him but he disappeared. Then I knew I had the power.
>
> 'If you gave me a cornet, I would play so loud that ships would hear me eight miles out at sea. That is how I was taught to play by Buddy Bolden. I can set type enough to run a newspaper. I can jump high enough to click my heels twice 'fore I touch down. I can dig a hole in the hard ground and fill it in after me, stay down there alive as long as I want. I went to fourth grade in school. I ain't no amnesia victim, but I don't remember anything about my people or anything else about myself. Tonight I'm going to divide myself with Neptune and maybe when you come back I will be able to tell you more. But, please tell everybody that I'm not going to hurt anyone, my spirit is just passing around Galveston Bay like a bird because I have been mistreated by the police.'

Police Chief Messina was contacted by the governor of the Insane Asylum at Jackson, Louisiana, who said that Schwab had escaped from there a fortnight earlier.

(Buddy Bolden, considered by many to be the originator of jazz, died in the asylum at Jackson in November 1931. He had been shut away for nearly twenty-five years. The hospital was racially segregated, so it is unlikely that Schwab would have had much contact with the cornettist. There is some evidence that Bolden played with a band of musical inmates; it is probable that Schwab heard him play.)

Messina was only too glad to return the nuisance to the custody of the asylum. The handcuffed prisoner was locked into the back of a patrol wagon to be delivered. However, just beyond Baton Rouge, on the road between Zachary and Slaughter, the wagon's engine failed. The two police officers in charge of the vehicle lifted the hood and were enveloped in a dense cloud of steam.

Realizing that they would be delayed for some time, the officers unlocked the back of the wagon so that the prisoner could stretch his legs – only to discover that the Devil Man had vanished.

□ □

The Homestead is part of a chain that covers the Southwest from Texas to California, and each restaurant looks virtually the same.

The design is straightforward: plate-glass windows on three sides of the dining area, with the kitchen and walk-in refrigerators at the back behind swinging doors. The customers sit in upholstered booths or at free-standing tables. There is a buffet counter that is filled with breakfast food – biscuits, sausage patties, bacon and homefries – from midnight until eleven and the rest of the day it is a salad bar. Mary Alice's job, beside waiting tables, was to make sure that the counter was stocked.

The laminated menu makes much of the Homestead's simplicity. The customer is supposed to be transported nostalgically to his grandmother's kitchen. I wondered how many grandmothers provided non-dairy creamer instead of milk. Once I made this point to Mary Alice and she told me that in rural east Texas and west Louisiana powdered milk is always served with coffee.

In keeping with the ersatz nostalgia, the waitresses wear checked gingham frocks and white aprons. Mary Alice clearly enjoyed the uniform; it allowed her to play a role. Despite the stiff hair and pancake make-up, she was quite convincing as the sexy *ingénue*; gasping at the stories the fishermen told her, leaning over as she poured their coffee; even her voice became higher and younger, the slur rendered childish, as if to imitate Marilyn Monroe.

It was a good act because, at the end of most shifts, her

tips were twice anyone else's, and some of the girls were half her age.

Mary Alice had two ardent admirers who only came to the Homestead when she was working; none of the other waitresses pleased them as much as she did. She made a clear distinction between admirers and potential sugarmen; admirers were kept at a distance. One of the admirers was a retired Jewish surgeon called Max Stern. I never met him but I did meet the other admirer, a portly youth called Monty Richardson, several times.

Monty was a senior at high school, who drove to the Homestead in a small green Datsun truck, and whiled away his afternoons telling Mary Alice blue jokes that she pretended not to understand; he kept one hand in his pocket most of the time.

I thought him a fat little creep and told Mary Alice so. She was more compassionate towards him. 'He ain't got no friends his own age. It's real sad. He won't go on the beach, he's so hulky. He's from a real respectable family and he's real clever; he's learnt a whole bunch of speeches, funny ones and political ones.'

Monty was a connoisseur of British television comedy: he had a collection of Benny Hill shows on videotape and his latest passion was *Are You Being Served?* which was broadcast on public television. He would recall his favourite scenes, laughing so much that it was difficult to understand him; he kept talking about 'wide-fronts', meaning Y-fronts. One day Monty asked if, when I returned to England, I would send him a selection of 'men's magazines': 'I bet those British men's magazines are *damn* fine.' Monty's other great interest was in Winston Churchill. In fact, he looked vaguely Churchillian.

The Homestead is next to a Ramada Inn and many of the customers are from the motel. That afternoon, sitting in a booth talking to Mary Alice, were a couple I would have guessed were in their late forties.

The man was small and thin, with very pitted skin and a large pink wart on the bridge of his nose. His blond hair was brushed forward over his ears, creating a mid-Sixties Mod effect, which seemed intentional. He wore metal-framed sunglasses and, despite the heat, a white leather coat, very tight across the chest; a burgundy shirt of some petroleum-derived fabric; brown slacks and pale zip-up suede boots. He was drinking coffee and smoking a panatella.

The woman (a mixture of ancestries producing an almost Egyptian look) was tall and thin. Her hair was scraped up beneath a black sombrero. She wore a crimson satin bomber jacket with *Simply The Best* emblazoned on the back, white jeans and red stilettos. Mary Alice was serving her a bottle of Michelob.

I guessed their car was air-conditioned and that they avoided going out in the sunshine. They certainly looked overdressed, and there was something mysterious, slightly vampirish, about both of them, as if they were nocturnal creatures unused to the daylight.

When Mary Alice saw me she called me over and introduced the woman. 'May I present Valma Curran from New Orleans, formerly lead *chanteuse* of the Valronas?' She pronounced it *shan-toose*.

'Mary Alice, honey, he ain't never heard of no Valronas!' She smiled – her teeth were long and dazzling – and offered her slender yellow hand (each finger bearing a large *diamanté* ring) for me to kiss rather than shake.

'Tell her, baby. You ain't never heard of no Valronas.'

'But I have. "You Left Without Leaving Your Address" . . .'

'Oo whee, fame!' Mary Alice put her hands on her hips.

Valma Curran looked quietly surprised. 'Where you hear that song?'

'I collect early soul, rhythm and blues.'

'Collect, huh?'

'Ooh child, now you're a collector's item!'

'It's a great song. Didn't Allen Toussaint produce it?'

'Un huh,' Valma shook her head, 'Marshall Sehorn.'

'What is a Valrona?' I asked, aware that it might be a silly question – what is a Shirelle, or a Vandella for that matter?

Valma smiled, tilting her head forward. 'Well, see, they was me, Valma, my baby sister Ronice, and our cousin Nadine, y'understand.'

She introduced her companion ('Have you met Jimmy Lee Swenson?'), who nodded begrudgingly in my direction.

Mary Alice went on, as if quoting some publicity handout. 'Jimmy Lee Swenson, personal celebrity management. Jimmy Lee, buddy of the stars.'

Jimmy Lee muttered. 'Yeah, yeah, yeah.' He looked uncomfortable. I asked if he was Valma's manager and he nodded. 'You could say that.'

Mary Alice said, 'Joseph's been studyin' local history. Knows all about them Karankawas . . .'

Valma was interested. 'Oh Lord! I heard they was can'bals!'

'Some people say that.'

'We had us a can'bal in New Orleans. Wasn't so long ago. The police found fifty pounds of human meat in his freezer!'

Mary Alice gasped. 'That is just awful.'

Jimmy Lee took up the story. 'It was a fellow from Chicago, settled on North Robinson Street. They found all these bags of spices and seasonin'. He was cookin' Chinese food!'

'Was he Chinese?' I asked.

'I don't think so. Guess Chinese is prob'ly the best way to serve human flesh.' Jimmy Lee yawned and stood up to leave.

He turned to Mary Alice. 'It was nice seein' you again, darlin'. I gotta rest. I'm headin' back to the motel.'

Then he patted Valma's shoulder and urged her to rest. 'Girl, remember the show starts at nine. It's nearly quarter of three now.'

To be honest, I couldn't think of any other songs by the Valronas. Presumably they still had a local following. I asked Valma if they sang often.

She shook her head. 'We played the Jazz Festival in 'seventy-six – that was the last time. And once we opened for Irma Thomas, 'bout that time. Ronice moved over to Seattle.' I asked if she was pursuing a solo career. 'Yeah, but it ain't singin'. I'm a magician.'

'Princess Valma! Voodoo Illusionist! Baby, where have y'all been?'

'Cabaret and shit,' explained Valma dismissively.

'And she fixes people!'

'That's on the side. They asks me to, I do what I can. I ain't promisin' them nothin'.'

Mary Alice was more enthusiastic. 'Oh, she's just modest. You got the power, child!'

Valma smiled and made a teetering gesture with her hand. 'I got it a little. Others, you better watch out. I do what I can.'

Mary Alice brought me some iced tea and we discussed this aspect of Valma Curran's career. I sensed that she was reticent but Mary Alice kept pushing her along. 'OK, Valma honey. Tell him how y'all saved Frankie Ullman's butt that time. Everybody thought he shoulda gone down. What was that you did, girl?'

'Aw, c'mon, Mary Alice.'

Mary Alice was insistent. 'Y'all want to hear this,' she told me.

'OK, OK. I got a beef tongue from a friend in the abbatoir. Then I wrote down all the names of the witnesses for the prosecution and the prosecutin' attorney on a little piece of paper, size of a dollar bill. Roll it like a tube. I cut a little slash in the tip of that beef tongue and I push that paper tube up into the slash. All the time Frankie Ullman's in court I got that tongue goin' round and round in the microwave. He walk outa there. Says they didn't even have a case.'

Mary Alice clapped her hands. 'There! Can y'all believe that?'

'Would that work if I was in trouble?' I asked Valma. It sounded useful.

'No, honey. It only work if you got the power.'

'Can you do all kinds of things like that?'

Valma giggled. 'All kinds, sure.'

Later, as the conversation entered magical realms, Valma told me a story, which her grandfather had told her, about an acquaintance of his from Greenville, Mississippi, a man called Cletus Pike, who worked, eighty years ago, on the river, until he grew tired of it and joined the crew of a ship leaving New Orleans for Jamaica.

The ship left New Orleans in the high summer, and that year it was especially hot and Cletus Pike, who was a famous river swimmer, would stare longingly at the blue water. The ship's mate, a man from the West Indies, warned Cletus Pike that swimming in that part of the ocean was dangerous, but Cletus Pike could not see why: the water looked clear and placid. The ship's mate warned that there were sharks. All day long Cletus Pike watched for sharks but saw none; deciding to take the risk, he jumped overboard. Within minutes he was surrounded by her-girls.

'What are her-girls?' I asked Valma.

'Her-girls? They half woman, half fish. Ain't you seen the movie *Splash*?'

'Mermaids.'

'Yeah, except the ones in this part of the ocean are called her-girls. That's what my grandaddy told me. You want me to carry on or you goin' to keep interruptin' me?'

Valma told me that the her-girls dragged Cletus Pike down to the bottom of the sea and questioned him. 'Greenville nigger, tell the truth, do you like fish?'

Cletus Pike was scared and did not know what to answer. After giving the matter some thought, he replied, 'If it's something to eat you wants to give me, if you'll please excuse me, I would like some pork chops or fried chicken wings. I just hate fish.'

Cletus Pike's answer pleased the her-girls, who clapped their hands and told him that if he had answered otherwise they would have summoned the sharks. Instead the her-girls announced, 'You are just the prettiest man we have seen in the water; we goin' to make you our king,' and they directed Cletus Pike to a ruined Spanish galleon that would serve as his palace. Cletus Pike lived in the galleon for a long time.

Once a year, on his birthday, he would swim back to New Orleans, then make his way up the Mississippi to Greenville. He would arrive at his parent's house, always wearing a green silk suit and a silvery cape, a beaver Homburg hat and alligator shoes with silver buckles. His pockets would be stuffed with pearls and gold and silver coins.

All his friends, among them Valma's grandfather, would look forward to Cletus Pike's birthday because he was a generous man who made sure that everybody shared his munificence. Consequently

Cletus Pike's parents, who had been poor, became rich, and they would hold celebration picnics to which a great many guests were invited. Chinese lanterns hung from the live oak trees, and there would be dancing – for Cletus Pike danced as gracefully and tirelessly as he swam – to the finest music; this was provided, in 1917, by Freddie Keppard's Olympia Orchestra; in 1922 Bessie Smith, the Empress of the Blues, sang with Charlie Johnson's Orchestra.

One year, on his thirty-second birthday, Cletus Pike saw that his mother had prepared a salad of canned salmon and mayonnaise. Cletus Pike said nothing; he turned and walked back to the river, and was never seen in Greenville again.

□ □

The *Santería* shop on 23rd Street was open. It was a small untidy place presided over by an old woman who watched me suspiciously. There were all kinds of candles in glass containers with inscriptions in Spanish and English: 'Law Stay Away', 'Lover Come To Me', 'Money Draw'; packets of coloured powder, statues of saints, aerosols, floor washes and beads; wallet-sized images of Saint Lazarus (on crutches, dogs licking his wounds) and Saint Expeditus (a Roman soldier) and the Virgins of Guadalupe and Cobré, the Seven African Powers and *La Mano Poderosa*, all with supplications printed on the back.

Santería was originally the Yoruba religion as it had survived in Cuba, a syncretism of African deities and Roman Catholic saints, spread across black and white cultures by miscegenation, so that it eventually became more associated with Hispanic than black culture, something that distinguishes *Santería* from Voodoo.

When Cuban immigrants came to Brooklyn and Miami, the cult spread further to attract Mexicans, Costa Ricans, Guatemalans, Hondurans and others, including American blacks. It is well established all along the Gulf Coast, which has strong links with both the Caribbean and Central America.

I bought a postcard of the Seven African Powers, and also

some Love Soap and some Fast Luck Soap, which I subsequently discovered were identical beneath their thrilling wrappers.

Mary Alice used Love Soap; and the scent that I took to be patchouli was actually Van Van, a very powerful voodoo oil that protected her from evil.

This superstitious awe struck me as a regional characteristic. In some cities – certainly in Houston and New Orleans – voodoo doctors still purvey amulets, charms and potions, made up individually for the customer.

The most costly amulet is a *gris-gris* (sometimes called a *mojo* or a *mojo hand*), which can be a single object (a piece of bone or a key) but is more often a leather or cloth pouch containing brick dust, yellow ochre, cayenne paper, possibly a dried lizard, or the foot of a hen, chanted over by the doctor, and supposedly deadly if placed beneath the threshold of an enemy's dwelling.

If you find a *gris-gris* you either die of fright or take it back to the voodoo doctor who will defuse the *gris-gris* for a large fee.

These doctors would seem to be in a position to make lots of money, but they are largely relics from the nineteenth century; they have been overtaken by fraudulent New Age healers.

The nineteenth century was voodoo's golden age. Then the most successful of the doctors were great showmen.

In the 1840s one such practitioner thrived in New Orleans, a huge man called Dr John whose face was covered with a spider-web tattoo. Dr John was not descended from slaves, he was a native of Senegal who had sailed to America of his own free will. By sheer intimidation, he persuaded domestic slaves to inform him of the affairs of their households, even to bring him diaries and letters. He went into business as a mind-reader, an omniscient wizard. His trademark magical trappings were an elephant's tusk and a bag of African shells; his *gris-gris* were pebbles that had been soaked in an oil extracted from snakes, frogs and lizards, then wrapped in a hank of human hair. He did have some formidable tricks; he could cause a shower of rocks to fall upon a victim.

Dr John amassed a fortune (by some estimates as much as $150,000), which he spent lavishly. He bought some land along the Bayou Road, where he built himself a house. When he was first well-known, he dressed in gaudy silken costumes, his fingers covered with diamond and emerald rings. Later, Dr John presented a more sombre, precise appearance: he wore white linen under a dark suit, a port-coloured military sash, and a black tricorne – worn to the side, in the Spanish fashion – adorned with a black ostrich plume. His landau was one of the finest in the South and sometimes he rode through town on a bright chestnut Tennessee Walker stallion. He acquired fifteen female slaves for his seraglio, and he fathered over fifty children; he officially married a white woman, a Swiss immigrant, but she bore him no legitimate children, for Dr John, who claimed to be a Bambara prince, despised mulattos.

For all his magnificence, Dr John had an Achilles' heel: he was illiterate. Nor had he any trust in banks; business transactions of any importance worried him; his lack of education left him vulnerable. Lafcadio Hearn, in his essay *The Last of the Voudoos?*, describes the doctor's decline:

> He was notoriously bad pay, and part of his property was seized at last to cover a debt. Then, in an evil hour, he asked a man without scruples to teach him how to write, believing that financial misfortunes were largely due to ignorance of the alphabet. After he had learned to write his name, he was innocent enough one day to place his signature by request at the bottom of a blank sheet of paper, and, lo! his real estate passed from his possession in some horribly mysterious way. Still he had some money left, and made heroic efforts to retrieve his fortunes. He bought other property, and he invested desperately in lottery tickets. The lottery craze finally came upon him, and had far more to do with his ultimate ruin than his losses in the grocery, the shoemaker's shop, and other establishments into which he had put several thousand dollars as the silent partner of people

> who cheated him. He might certainly have continued to make a good living, since people still sent for him to cure them with his herbs, or went to see him to have their fortunes told, but all his earnings were wasted in tempting fortune. After a score of seizures and a long succession of evictions, he was at last obliged to seek hospitality from some of his numerous children; and of all he had once owned nothing remained to him but his African shells, his elephant's tusk, and the sewing-machine table that had served him to tell fortunes and to burn wax candles upon.

There were two other noted voodoo doctors in the Crescent City.

In 1861 a slave called Washington set himself up as the Mighty Doctor Yah-Yah. His great panacea was a mixture of Jamestown (possibly jimson) weed, sulphur and honey, to be sipped from a glass that had been rubbed against a black cat with one white foot. This marvellous brew granted wishes, cured baldness and impotence as well as skin diseases, and it rendered drinkers irresistible to the object of their affections.

A Corsican tailor sipped rather too much of the stuff and was treated for poisoning. The Mighty Doctor Yah-Yah was brought before the magistrates, and his owner fined $15. Thereafter the Mighty Doctor retired to work as a field-hand.

The best-selling love-charms were provided by Dr Jack. They were beef hearts, studded with cloves, wrapped in scented white crêpe. These charms cost $20 each, a considerable sum at the time. In his later years Dr Jack was an invalid. A large beef heart was nailed to the wall above his bed, and some visitors claimed that it actually throbbed. On 10 June 1869 Dr Jack died; the heart dropped from the wall onto his pillow.

□ □

Henry Glover shambled along Mechanic Street in a flapping grey coat, grey smoke pouring from his nose and mouth. Had he found a gallery that would exhibit his pictures?

'No, baby, no. Everything transpires to greet my disappointment. This has been the way for as far back as my memory extends. Why? The system. The system dictates false criterions. Necessarily a creative artist must struggle. I agree, you know what I mean? But how long? There lies the opportunity for cowards – they are cowards – to cover their weakness. Come see us in a year! What the hell! These paintings cannot be improved. They are flowerings . . .'

He had been sleeping on the ruined back seat of his car, making more pictures with pastels on dalerboard. He was on his way to discuss some temporary work, to finance a move to California. The combined smells of nicotine and (the mysterious) seaweed were overbearing. The rejection had upset him so much that he rambled. My presence allowed him the shallowest pretence that he was talking to somebody other than himself.

'What I need to know is . . . what do they intend? Any word read or heard only conveys the meaning that is available to the person reading or hearing it from his individual understanding of the word and that meaning is based on the values that his entire life's experiences have brought to that word up to that instant. You can't *be* sure, man.'

'Don't take it personally. The galleries have to play safe, it's a precarious business.'

'Precarious? They are employed by the Bechtel Corporation. They're shipping in poisoned roaches, poisoned ants and bees in any of those containers and they have made them in Washington laboratories. I know this – I have access to such classified information – don't ask me how I know this. The concept is so simple: make war on the poor. As an artist I am undermined by poverty, continually . . .'

Henry Glover left in an angry cloud of smoke.

In the second-hand bookshop I found a paperback edition of *The Soul Of The Ape & The Soul Of The White Ant* by Eugène Marais.

Then I rode through the various parts of town that were considered unsafe but I saw nothing alarming; I noticed a hairdresser's called *Aggressive Beauty Salon*, and lots of graffiti to indicate the presence of gangs – not that any were about. It was terribly hot. There were lots of massage parlours and martial-arts studios. I headed back towards the beach.

On my way I passed somebody I recognized from the years I spent in Austin, who was standing outside the Gulf Coast Maxillo-Facial Surgery. I could not recall his first name although I was certain that his surname was Willard; all I could remember was that he came to a party that Nadia and I gave, uninvited, climbed onto our roof and threw up. We had to live with the smell until the rain washed the sick away. Now Willard was evidently a doctor and my reminiscence was likely to embarrass him, so I rode on.

I swam again in the warm brown sea, then sat on one of the rock jetties reading about chacma baboons.

□ □

On the sea-wall opposite Speedy Gonzales, Henry Glover was talking, in an excited staccato, to a tall, patrician, middle-aged man. The conversation was rather one-sided. The tall man listened intently to Henry's rambling. His neat black hair was greying at the temples; the structure of his jaw seemed exaggerated; at first glance, he looked like a film star of the late 1950s, the George Hamilton type.

Closer scrutiny, however, revealed small far-apart eyes beneath jet-black brows and a wide, flattened nose. It was almost a pre-Columbian face, with a terracotta complexion, certainly handsome but less of a stereotype than I had first supposed. He was wearing expensive clothes: a stiff white sailcloth shirt and bright madras Bermuda shorts, with black penny loafers. Around his left wrist was a heavy silver bracelet inlaid with turquoise.

Henry Glover nodded to me and introduced his companion as Mr Guadalupe from Houston. Mr Guadalupe shook my hand disinterestedly and continued listening to Henry Glover, leaning forward slightly and nodding. The sun was going down.

I went into Speedy Gonzales. Mr Mendoza sat at one of the tables doing some paperwork. He had had a good day: there had been a run on his Original Pumpkin Seed Salads. Vanessa brought me some *chalupas* and a salad of iceberg lettuce.

A few minutes later Mr Guadalupe came into the restaurant and sat at a table quite near mine. 'As it happens, my friend, I collect . . .' he announced confidentially, as if he needed to explain why he had been talking to Henry Glover.

Mr Guadalupe had an oleaginous voice; it was difficult to place his accent but clearly it wasn't southern (it reminded me of Dick Dastardly's voice in *The Wacky Races*). 'Outsider Art . . . *Art Brut* . . . call it what you will . . . is very, very collectable nowadays. My personal taste runs to the more polished – Florine Stettheimer, that kind of thing . . . but I can trade, the wilder side's terribly *in*. Basquiat, all that . . . I was looking at the *dreck* on show down here when in walks this . . . this apparition . . . Of course, they don't know what to make of him. Whereas I could tell . . . at a glance. Oh, my dear, the poor creature was fuming . . . Best not to interfere when someone's in that state . . .'

Vanessa brought him a rather bloody *fajita*. Mr Guadalupe looked happily at the piece of skirt steak and ran his tongue along his upper teeth, which were unnaturally straight and white, in keeping with the whole outdated glamour of his appearance.

'I was just popping in here for a bite before *schlepping* home, when who should I bump into?'

Mr Guadalupe started eating in an unexpectedly messy way, cramming bits of meat and flour tortilla into his mouth. His jaw clicked as he chewed.

'Hopeless, of course . . . If you ask me, he's not really interested in selling. The most extraordinary ideas . . . he wants a travelling show to go around the inner cities . . . I asked, couldn't I buy just one or two of the pictures? Show them to people . . . make him a bit of a name? Out of the question, he says. I explained that I happen to be a personal friend of the Menils – he couldn't find a better contact – the flattest refusal!'

He finished the *fajita*. 'Do you know, I'm still peckish.' Mr Guadalupe ordered a hamburger without fries, asking Vanessa to make sure the patty wasn't overcooked: 'I prefer all meat *au jus*.'

'You couldn't persuade him for me, could you? You obviously have a rapport . . . I'll leave you my card . . . I couldn't be easier to reach.'

The card said: David Guadalupe, LUPE DESIGN, 1301 Bissonnet, Houston.

'We do interiors mostly,' he explained. 'You'd like our work, it's retro *moderne* . . . you know, Syrie Maugham . . .' There was a smear of *guacamole* on his cheek.

'Of course, I'm often down this way . . . I'm drawn . . . My people were from these parts, for generations . . . That might have something to do with the attraction.'

I asked Mr Guadalupe if he was born in Galveston. He wiped his face. 'Oh no. Burbank, California. My papa was in the movies, played Indians . . . That was in the 1930s. Good work, too. He was born in Mexico . . . but Daddy always maintained that his family were from this part of the world . . . Karankawas, you see. That's why we're all so tall . . . all the Guadalupe men are over six foot.'

The hamburger arrived. Mr Guadalupe devoured it in three mouthfuls. As he was getting up to leave, he urged me again. 'Persuade our friend to reconsider, please . . . to get in touch with me. Quite honestly, how many breaks like this is he likely to get?'

I told Mr Guadalupe I would try but I was doubtful I could be any help. 'He's in a world of his own,' I said.

'Who was that wise guy? A realtor?' asked Mr Mendoza, after Mr Guadalupe had left. 'Everybody's tryin' to sell property down here.'

'No, he collects pictures.'

'Then why didn't he buy my picture? Fifty bucks.'

'I think he collects paintings.'

'Then he's in the wrong town. Property, that's another story.'

I asked Mr Mendoza about the pier that was for sale. 'What do you think they'll do, turn it into a restaurant?'

'You ask me, that's a state monument. You ever hear about the Maceos?'

§

Throughout the 1920s two brothers, Sicilian immigrants, Salvatore (Sam) and Rosario (Rose) Maceo, worked as hairdressers on Market Street. The brothers had come to America at the turn of the century, when Sam was six and Rose was thirteen. Their parents had settled in Leesville, Louisiana. After attending beauty college in New Orleans, Sam and Rose struck out for Galveston in 1910.

The State of Texas endorsed the Prohibition amendment and, from April 1918, Galveston was officially dry. Almost immediately bootleggers recognized that Galveston was an ideal place for smuggling; high-quality foreign alcohol was a more desirable commodity than the bath-tub gin that many bootleggers provided.

Typically shipments loaded in Canada were shipped to British Honduras, then reloaded onto large freighters that anchored some forty miles out at sea from Galveston, beyond American jurisdiction.

The bootleggers brought the liquor ashore from the freighters in small boatloads, which they loaded onto railway cars, to be distributed across a network of bootleggers covering the South and the Midwest.

The island had its resident hoodlums: the Beach Gang, led by Dutch Voight and Ollie Quinn, and the Downtown Gang, headed by George Musey and Johnny Jack Nounes.

The Beach Gang unloaded their liquor on the deserted western beaches of the island. Sam and Rose Maceo joined the Beach Gang, initially on a very small scale. They provided cheap red wine for their customers at the salon, which they bought from Ollie Quinn. Later Quinn asked the hairdressers to hide larger amounts of liquor for him. When the Maceos became aware of the profits involved, they invested their savings of $1,500 in the Beach Gang.

The Downtown Gang was a more flamboyant operation. Johnny Jack Nounes, who always wore a large diamond stickpin, kept $1 million in his personal bank account. He was arrested twice by the Federal Bureau of Investigation.

On the second occasion, in 1928, his partner George Musey was also convicted. Musey skipped his $10,000 bail and fled to Montreal. His Canadian contact was Big Jim Clark. Clark did not get on with the renegade Texan.

Shortly after Musey's arrival, Clark, through spite, informed the Beach Gang of a consignment worth $210,000 sent out by Musey. Instead of being met by the Downtown Gang, the liquor was hijacked by the Beach Gang. There followed a gun battle on the streets of Galveston that led to Dutch Voight's arrest. Shortly afterwards, in Montreal, both Musey and Clark were arrested.

That left Ollie Quinn as the most senior bootlegger in Galveston. Quinn was getting old and he was happy to pass on his business to the Maceos. He could see that the brothers had brains beyond the shallow bluster of ordinary hoodlums.

From the first the Sicilians were more ambitious than their Irish and German colleagues, more committed and ruthless. Within a few years of heading the Beach Gang, they had driven the Downtown Gang off the island.

The Maceos instinctively understood corruption; it was easy enough to square the local authorities. They took stock of their situation. As more Texans bought their own cars, Galveston was benefiting from a surge in tourism. The Maceos switched the focus of their operation from liquor to gambling. They opened the Hollywood Dinner Club.

Two younger brothers, Vincent and Frank Maceo, had joined the operation; as would, over the years, any number of cousins and in-laws.

The Hollywood Dinner Club was the first air-conditioned nightclub in America. Lavish food was prepared by French chefs and served by French waiters. The decor was tropical, banana trees shaded the entrance. The most popular entertainers (Sophie Tucker, the Ritz Brothers) and the hottest dance bands (Guy Lombardo and his Royal

Canadians, Ray Noble) drew the crowds. The greatest attraction of all was the illegal back-room casino.

The Maceos had invented the formula that later entrepreneurs would use in Las Vegas and Atlantic City. The Hollywood Dinner Club operated, undisturbed by the law, for sixteen years.

The brothers became very rich men in the hardest of times. Beside the Hollywood, they owned the Studio Lounge, the Turf Athletic Club, the Western Room and the Moulin Rouge. More cousins and relatives moved to Galveston to help them with their enterprise. The Studio Lounge was the concern of Victor 'the Gigolo' Maceo. He also ran a restaurant on the mainland, the Chili Bowl in Kemah.

There was another cousin called Victor Maceo, who became known as 'Little Vic' to avoid confusion; he was never given a specific job because he was not very bright; he had no business sense so he ran errands for the others. Little Vic would proudly tell people that he was designated a 'General' by the syndicate: the title sounded grand and powerful – it meant that he was a general functionary.

Galveston gained a reputation for raffish pleasures when the Maceos ran the town. The syndicate allowed other casinos to operate as long as their owners understood that they existed at the Maceos' pleasure. The bordellos on Postoffice Street were under no obligation to the Maceos but the madams had the sense to ban gambling on their premises.

Legitimate businesses benefited from the surge in tourism. 'The Free State of Galveston' was the most enticing resort on the Gulf Coast. Not a single bank closed in Galveston during the Depression. There were jobs for everyone. Hotels were full, even in winter.

Nobody was going to prosecute the Maceos, who were quickly becoming respected public figures. Sam had a family pew at St Mary's Cathedral. The syndicate supported charities and awarded unofficial university scholarships.

They also made sure there was no unpleasantness on the island.

Particularly successful gamblers were always escorted back to their hotels by bodyguards, lest they should be robbed on the way.

When one of their heavies, Leo Lera, had too much to drink on Christmas Eve, 1938, and shot a patron, Harry Phillips, it was Vic the Gigolo who personally delivered him to police headquarters. Lera was found guilty of murder and executed.

There were many who feared – and some who hoped – that the Lera case would close down the Maceo's empire but he seems to have been a sacrificial victim.

As far as law and order went, the brothers made a great show of helping the police; they employed a vigilante patrol (Rose's Night Riders) to scare petty criminals off the island.

The Maceos bought a pleasure pier, jutting out over the Gulf. Over the years they ran a succession of restaurants on the pier: the Chop Suey, the Grotto, the Sui Jen. Sam Maceo took an interest in restaurant design; he would get ideas from his visits to New York and Los Angeles, and he would change the name of an establishment whenever he changed the decor.

In 1942 the syndicate decided to close the Hollywood Dinner Club altogether and open a new club on the pier. The name of the new club would be the Balinese Room. The food would remain Chinese, for the celebrated head chef, Go Bo (who had been General Pershing's cook in the First World War), had fans across the state and had become indispensable.

At the entrance to the pier was a door with a hidden metal detector; all the male guests were discreetly screened. Past the door was a 400-foot walkway along to the Balinese Room.

The room itself was a riot of South Seas decor. The waiters had cut fishing-holes into the floor and walls of the restaurant and would sometimes stop their immaculate service to pull up a snapper or mudshark. Customers often took over the manning of these holes, which became an added attraction.

As at the previous club, the greatest draw of all was the casino, a more high-powered affair than before. Gamblers came from all over the South and Southwest; wealthy Houstonians, oilmen, even the occasional state governor, could be found at the tables.

Galvestonians themselves were discouraged from playing at the casino because the Maceos did not want their neighbours to lose too much. The consideration did not extend to the numbers racket, which, in 1939, made $300,000 from the island population alone.

By all accounts, the Maceos were honest proprietors who ran a clean game. Throughout the war the casino made a profit of $4 million a year.

The only entrance was from the shore. Should there be a raid by the Texas Rangers (the county police left the Maceos alone), the casino staff had a few minutes in which to remove the roulette wheels and convert the roulette tables into billiard tables before the Rangers blustered through the restaurant; a drill was rehearsed daily so that the exercise could be accomplished with speed and efficiency.

Sometimes, mocking the lawmen's efforts, the orchestra would strike up 'The Eyes Of Texas', and the diners and dancers and gamblers all laughed.

Eventually, in 1951, the Chief Ranger, Colonel Homer Garrison, grew tired of having his force ridiculed by the Maceos and arranged for Ranger Clint Peoples to operate undercover.

Disguising himself as Mr Robert Eberling, a rancher from Johnson City, Ranger Peoples booked a room for himself and his wife at the Buccaneer Hotel. Ranger Peoples went regularly to the casino; he occupied himself with the dice and roulette tables while Mrs Peoples played the fruit machines.

Ranger Peoples discovered the metal detector at the door, and that it was not activated when women passed through; it would therefore be possible to sneak his badge and pistol into the casino in his wife's handbag.

At the precise moment the Texas Rangers made their raid on the pier, Ranger Peoples produced his badge and pistol. He announced that he was arresting the twelve casino employees.

The fines were relatively light but the raid garnered a lot of bad publicity for the Balinese Room; people stopped coming in such droves.

Later the same year the Texas House of Representatives authorized an investigation into organized crime in the state. It was revealed that in the fiscal year of 1950 the Maceos had earned $827,764 from slot machines, $349,267 from racing bets, $830,586 from the club rooms, $267,689 from drink sales, $122,817 from tip books, $21,895 from baseball pools and $91,055 from bingo. The Maceos realized that their empire was no longer inviolable.

Sensing panic, the Texas Rangers increased the pressure. Although the Balinese Room continued to operate, the strain started to tell. Ever more customers stayed away.

The Texas Rangers discovered a warehouse containing 350 slot machines, which they sledgehammered and dumped in the bay. The mayor of Galveston was furious, claiming that the Texas Rangers were endangering shipping.

Another 2,000 machines were discovered and destroyed at the old Hollywood Dinner Club. That was the end of the Maceos' business.

Sam died of a heart attack in 1961.

In 1965, shortly after Rose's death, the Balinese Room was sold at auction.

The other Maceos drifted away, to Houston, or out of state. Little Vic stayed on the island, running a motel on 88th and Seawall Boulevard.

Vic the Gigolo's son now works for the County Sheriff's Department. He has been decorated several times for bravery.

In the spring of 1993, Little Vic was eighty-nine years old. For fourteen years he had been a widower. He no longer ran the motel.

On 3 February, he was drinking coffee with Mr Mendoza at Randall's on 61st Street. They had a special discount for senior citizens. El Gran Queso, who lived on 61st Street, often took advantage of it on his walk to work. He liked talking with the old-timers, remembering the golden days of radio comedy.

Little Vic was wearing a dark pin-striped suit, a striped shirt with the collar open, a gold chain and a fedora hat. In his old age he tended to play up his gangster past but nobody took him very seriously.

Mr Mendoza thought Little Vic was senile; the old man kept on and on about a certified public accountant called Pete Miller, who, he claimed, owed him money from a real-estate transaction. What had happened was that Miller (who had once worked at the Balinese Room as a busboy and also as a cashier at the Studio Lounge) had bought a house from Little Vic in 1968 for $45,000; in 1991 Miller had sold the house for $240,000. Little Vic, unable to grasp the rise in property values over twenty-five years, felt sure that he had been cheated.

El Gran Queso tried to explain to him that nothing crooked had taken place.

Little Vic could not be pacified; it made his blood boil that a member of the Maceo family should be swindled by one of their busboys.

That Wednesday morning, when Little Vic left Randall's, he drove his red sports car to the building on 22nd and Broadway where the accountant practised.

On walking into the office, he confronted Pete Miller, who poured the old man some coffee and offered to go over all the documents relating to the transaction.

Little Vic drew a .38 revolver from beneath his jacket and shot Miller in the arm.

The police would remark that both the weapon and the bullets were antiques.

When Little Vic was arrested in the car park, he looked at the young officer sternly – Mr Mendoza imitated the old man – and complained, 'You do not handcuff a gentleman in this town!'

MARY ALICE AND I WERE SITTING AT FENTON'S FAMOUS FOR NOTHING, a combined café and bait camp on the bayside shore, eating shrimp po-boys and onion rings and listening to Dorothy Moore singing 'Misty Blue'. Mary Alice had finished the day shift at the Homestead and she was very tired so I had driven the Impala across the peninsula.

When we came to the crossroads at Highway 87 I discovered that the brakes did not work. 'It's OK, they been like that a couple of weeks. You just click down into that first and let the engine stall.' I could not work out how to do that but we were fortunate, there was nobody else at the crossroads.

At Fenton's a rickety deck overlooks the bay and the Intracoastal Waterway. Selwyn, the proprietor, grew up in Liverpool and, although he had not been there for forty-five years, there was still a trace of scouse in his accent.

I asked if he wanted to go back.

'Nope. Wouldn't be the same. Too many niggros and Palestinians.' I think he meant Pakistanis.

Great big ships moved slowly by; some were quite rusty and it looked as if particles of rust were sifting off onto the surface of the water, colouring the slipstream. When the tide splashed against the legs of the deck, globules of iridescent oil broke into smaller globules, like the eyes of cuttlefish.

Mary Alice told me that she planned to stop drinking so much, she felt that it was time to settle down. 'Gonna find me a veterinarian, that's what I want. To help him cure those little dogs and kitties. Live in a little white house and be a veterinary nurse. I could train.'

'Couldn't you settle down with Captain Guidry?'

'He wants me to. Seems to me he lacks romance. I ain't in love with him, put it that way.'

'Why do you drink so much?'

It was a question that bemused both of us with its frankness. As soon as I asked, I wished that I hadn't. In the few seconds of silence that followed the question, I found myself guessing her answer.

She might say, honestly, that she drank no more than anyone else in the company she kept.

She might raise her defences and say that as long as she kept her life together and hurt nobody, it was up to her how she spent her wages.

Instead she brushed some hair away from her eyes and made a child's serious face. 'I don't know any more, Joseph. I useda think it made sad things funny; you know, it let y'all stand back from your life. That's what I useda tell myself. Only now I'm right in the middle of my life and there's no way of standin' back, like it or leave it. And the sad things are real sad and all the time. So I guess, it sounds funny but it's true, it's to keep from cryin'.'

I said I knew what she meant: there are flashes when one sees the actual squalor of one's existence. Equally there are less frequent flashes of great reassurance when the chaos is revealed to be part of an intricate benevolent design; I call them Flashes of Mercy.

Mary Alice nodded. 'What I am drinkin' for is that mercy. It used to work till I wore it out.'

'Love can chase any black dog away.' Fittingly, there was a Marvin Gaye song floating out from the kitchen: he was singing about love in a high prophetic voice. 'Have you ever been in love?'

That was what I was going to ask Mary Alice earlier. The question about drinking had shot in front.

'Sure, I was in love with Elvis Presley and Grizzly Adams,' she replied pertly. I had never heard of Grizzly Adams. Mary Alice explained that he was a television character.

She told me about a second encounter with Elvis.

In 1976 Mary Alice had a sugarman called Randall Howitzer. Howitzer was a millionaire, 'a big butter-and-egg man' from Memphis, but he was different from her other sugarmen in that his fortune was inherited – 'so he was kinda aristocratic'. Howitzer avoided the world of commerce; he spent his time studying Theosophy, the works of Krishnamurti, Madame Blavatsky and C. W. Leadbetter.

'Randall had the soul of a poet, a real spiritual nature. He useda read cards and all that – gave me that *Cheiro's Book of Numbers* but I never could get to work it.'

Mary Alice had asked Howitzer if he knew Elvis as soon as she discovered he came from Memphis. Howitzer had replied that he was a frequent visitor to Graceland, for Elvis Presley shared his interest in the Occult.

That summer Howitzer's wife, Suzy, took their twin daughters off to Europe and, during their absence, he asked Mary Alice to stay with him in Memphis.

'Oh, Joseph, they had the most beautiful home. Right there in the lobby was a big old golden Buddha smilin' down.' (She pronounced it *Booder*.) 'Well, I just rushed over and patted his belly for luck. Instead of doors, every room had those bead curtains hangin' and the whole place smelt real fine because there was incense burnin' everywhere.

'Randall had gotten keen on that *I Ching* and one Friday night he sat up real late tossin' those coins from a leather cup. He was just completely absorbed. About three o'clock he wakes me up and he's real pallid, sayin', "Mary Alice, unless I'm mistaken, old Elvis is in real danger. It looks as if he could be askin' Saint Peter for a passport within twelve months." So I said we had to contact him, let him know, and Randall says he reckons Elvis got more of a handle on this stuff than he does, and there ain't nothin' he's been told that Elvis don't know long since.

'Well, the next day we went shoppin', Randall bein' of a mind to give me somethin' to remember him by after his wife gets back, and we headed for downtown Memphis. There was a whole mass of folk throngin' the doorway of a jeweller's store and Randall says to me, "Y'all can guess who they got in there," when out comes Elvis himself and the crowd starts hollerin'. He's got the manager of the store with him and the manager's holdin' out a big old velvet tray covered with fine rings. What struck me, maybe in the light of that darn *I Ching*, I just don't know, was how ill and lost Elvis was lookin'. He was wearin' all those tight black Chinesey clothes and he was sweatin' up and there was a rash on his cheeks and neck where he'd been shavin' with a blunt razor and you couldn't see his eyes behind those mirrors. I called out to him but I couldn't tell if he remembered me even. His mouth was all hangin' down and slobbery like he was slow-witted.

'Do you know what he was doin'? He was handin' out those rings just like little party favours and, honey, I know some of them sapphires and rubies gotta be worth $4,000 or more. And the people in the crowd were trashy old local people, clawin' out for what they could get; I could tell they didn't have no love in their hearts for Elvis. Randall and I just watched dumbstruck.

'I asked him what he made of it and he said, "Reckon that old boy knows he don't got cause to hold onto his money." But to me it was pitiful. And that was the last time I ever saw him.'

I wanted to know what had happened to the condominium in Dallas; I had been wondering what made her move to Bolivar.

'Truth is, Joseph, it kinda dissolved on me. You know, like in those movies, when a dream ends and the whole picture just wobbles. Next thing I knew, it was gone.'

What about Billy Bob Edelman?

'He's still up there.'

Mary Alice did not elaborate. Instead she told me about the time she smuggled a parrot across the Mexican border inside a Crown Royal box.

I was looking across the bay to Texas City. Selwyn came out with two more longnecks. He told me that in 1947 Texas City had exploded.

On 16 April, just after dawn, longshoremen were loading a French ship, the *Grandcamp*, with 100-lb sacks of ammonium nitrate, to be used as fertiliser. One of the hatches was smoking. The longshoremen discovered a small fire and poured two buckets of water onto the flames.

As the fire resisted dowsing, they tried a fire extinguisher, again to no avail, so they turned a hose onto the fire. The first mate of the *Grandcamp* thought the pressure of the hose would damage the cargo; he ordered the smoking hatch closed and attempted to subdue the fire with steam. The lid of the hatch was blown off.

The crew abandoned the ship and the first mate called the Texas City Volunteer Fire Department. Tawny smoke was billowing from the ship and burning paper sacks wafted through the sky.

At nine there was a terrific explosion and the *Grandcamp* was torn to pieces. A black and orange fire-ball rose up and blotted out the sun. A 15-foot wave rocked across the bay and two small aeroplanes dropped from the sky like shot ducks. Pieces of the ship were thrown as far as 13,000 feet. A 20-ton section of deck flew 2,000 feet through the air.

Every house within a mile of the ship was blown down. The Texas City Volunteer Fire Department was lost in the blast. Fortunately a strong north wind blew the poisonous fumes away from the city.

Pieces of red-hot debris pierced the gas tanks of the oil refineries, causing more explosions. Selwyn was watching it happen.

'Flames from her caught the Monsanto Chemical Company, then Stone Oil, then Republic and Richardson. That whole place was a damn wall of flame.' The explosions continued all through the day. Firemen and medics rushed to the scene from Houston and Galveston.

At one in the morning a second ship, the *High Flyer*, exploded. 'It was like a rainbow, made of fireworks. Them coloured lines shootin' out, crossin' the bay.'

A neighbouring ship, the *Wilson B. Keene*, was split neatly in two. The turbine of the *High Flyer*, weighing four tons, was discovered 4,000 feet away.

The death toll reached 512 (399 bodies were identified, 113 were counted as missing). The seriously injured numbered 1,784 and 539 buildings were destroyed. 'It was a national disaster and I seen it all from this side of the bay,' declared Selwyn proudly.

Mary Alice drove the Impala back along Loop 108 – I was reluctant to drive a car with no brakes.

We crossed Horseshoe Lake and saw Happy Jack and Ronny Sue fishing. Mary Alice honked and waved and Ronny Sue waved back.

'All they do is fish,' said Mary Alice. 'I told Sparling he ain't got nothin' to worry about, in my opinion. Soon as Cockerdoody dies, Happy Jack'll head on back to Houston.'

'What does he do there?'

'Baby, I don't know. I heard he lives in back of a fun palace. Locks the place, does a little sweepin' out.'

'What is a fun palace?'

'You know, video games.'

Lucan came to the House of Blue Lights that evening. He announced: 'I'm gone do me some beach-drivin'. Y'all comin' or what?'

Mary Alice and I got into the truck beside him and we sped along Highway 87.

Lucan turned to me. 'Old Sparling says you lookin' to buy a truck.'

I denied the rumour.

Lucan laughed. 'Man, I'll sell you this one for fifteen hundred.'

'How's your uncle doin'?' asked Mary Alice, uncomfortable, I could tell, with the speed.

'Catfish is sittin' there with the old buzzard. His mind's gone, I reckon. Keeps on askin' for Lucky Paradise. You remember him?'

'I surely do, but I don't think he's alive. If he is he's gotta be a hundred years old.'

'No, baby, him and Cockerdoody are the same age; maybe Lucky's a year older, no more.'

We pulled up with a screech ('How do you like them brakes?') at the Horseshoe Liquor and Meat Mart so that Lucan could get a bottle of whisky. Mary Alice offered to pay for it. Lucan would not hear of it. 'Baby, you keep your money.'

Mary Alice found a Chris Ledoux tape under the seat and put it on. Lucan was in the shop a long time. The Horseshoe Liquor and Meat Mart was run by Spike and Garland, two sturdy homosexuals who had met in the navy. They were both in their forties and well-liked. Spike had received the Purple Heart (as had Catfish) and he walked with a stick. Garland bred Affenpinschers, tiny, flat-faced black dogs like spider-monkeys, that scurried in a troop around his bare feet. They also kept a peacock in an enclosure beside the store.

I asked Mary Alice if their lifestyle met with local disapproval. Apparently they were tolerated. In the early 1970s, the police raided the Kontiki, a gay club on the island, and thirty-nine men were arrested for indecency. Spike was one of them. The opinion in Port Bolivar was that the police were victimizing the discreet behaviour of a war hero.

Mary Alice called Spike and Garland 'the boys' and they sometimes allowed her credit. Besides selling liquor and meat, they rented out videos.

I asked Mary Alice who Lucky Paradise was. She told me that he was a country singer who had grown up on the peninsula and, for many years, he was Cockerdoody's best friend. I asked if he was famous. 'Well, yeah but, you know, back when my daddy was growin' up. He would have quit years ago.'

Lucan came back to the truck. 'Garland says Trudi keeps in touch with Lucky. You ever see her, baby?'

'Why, surely. She cleans the rooms at Pirate's Cove.'

'Still does, huh?'

Soon we were on the beach. The moon was huge and full and the sky was clear and starry and we could see the lights of Crystal Beach ahead of us and, out at sea, the lights of ships.

Lucan was doing at least a hundred. Sometimes the truck left the ground. He smiled over at me. 'I tell you, boy, this sucker hauls ass.' I did not say much because I was terrified. Mary Alice was holding on to the door handle and her eyes were shut.

We stopped suddenly, spinning as the wheels jammed in the sand. Another truck was stuck in the wetter sand at the water's edge; a man and a woman stood beside it.

'Y'all need towin'?' called Lucan.

'That or we gone call a wrecker,' answered the man. 'Damn tide's comin' in.'

'I got boards and a rope,' offered Lucan. 'Wrecker's gone cost you at least seventy-five dollars. I'll get you outta there for forty.'

Moving the truck proved no easy task. Lucan and the man kept arguing about the correct procedure. Mary Alice and I stood to one side.

The woman walked over to us. She had a little hairbrush with which she would brush her hair up from underneath, puffing it out into a soft blond cloud. She was extremely thin so the hairstyle made her look like a dandelion.

'You have real pretty hair,' Mary Alice told her.

'I know. It's my best feature,' answered the woman tensely. 'This sea air flattens it. Normally I carry some spray.'

'Don't worry, darlin'. You'll be home soon.'

'I am worried. Real worried. I am in deep shit,' she told us. 'My husband's gone kill me now.'

'Just because your hair's a little lifeless?'

'Got nothin' to do with my damn hair!' She was all on edge.

'He'll calm down, honey. Men get real childish around trucks. I can tell your husband's a gentleman deep down.'

'That *ain't* my husband,' whined the woman. Mary Alice had the wrong end of the stick. 'My husband drives a big old sixteen-wheeler. He'll have gotten home a couple of hours ago.'

When we got back I walked along to Pirate's Cove to use the telephone. I wanted to speak to a friend in New Orleans, where I was heading next. I had been trying to get hold of her since my arrival in the United States. Every time I rang I got onto her answerphone.

Parked in front of the motel was a red truck full of very dusty Chicanos eating corn chips and drinking Schlitz Malt Liquor.

Around the buzzing neon sign swarmed thousands of pale moths.

One of the Chicanos was playing a guitar and singing a song with the repeated phrase '*tu corazon traidor*' that sounded to me like a translation of Hank Williams' 'Your Cheatin' Heart' and I stood by the telephone listening until he had finished the song; by which time the Chicanos were eating apricots, or very small peaches, spitting the stones down by the side of the red truck.

My friend was not at home. It was eleven o'clock at night, too late to try again.

I went back along Loop 108. Some sizeable creature splashed about in the marsh but I could not see anything through the reeds. I wondered if it was an alligator.

I asked Mary Alice if it could have been one and she replied half-teasingly, 'Maybe so, honey. I heard that noise too. I put on some of y'all's Jungle Repellant. That should work.'

I lay on my sofa, listening to the frogs and the cats, and the alligator seemed a comfortable menace, like the cold air around a warm bed on a winter's night. I felt very peaceful.

In the middle of the night I heard Sparling settling down directly beneath my room. He was singing, softly and solemnly, a slow violent song that sounded hundreds of years old:

'I took her by her golden curls and drug her round and round,
Throwin' her into the river that flows through Knoxville town.
Go down, go down, you Knoxville girl,
With your dark and rovin' eye.
Go down, go down, you Knoxville girl.
You can never be my bride.'

There was an eerie contrast between the tune, which might have been a lullaby, and the frank brutality of the lyric.

Seven

I HAD BOUGHT TEN BLUE LIGHT BULBS IN GALVESTON AND I WAS STANDING on a chair on the deck, replacing the dead ones. It was late morning, clear and very hot already.

Sweet William kept panting although he had a big bowl of water. He was rarely comfortable away from Mary Alice, fretting dreadfully until she was within sight. For weeks he had hidden from me. Now he no longer hid but he watched me with constant apprehension.

Princess was walking back from Pirate's Cove. She was on the other side of the marsh, tying her red hair back with a rubber band, floating along behind her balloon. I waved to her. She lifted her eyes and clucked her tongue (as if to say 'That was what I expected you to do') and when she got nearer she called up, 'You all wanta drive me to the Moody Gardens?'

The name appealed to me; I imagined live oaks festooned with

Spanish moss, shadows on the water, and bridges – with any luck, a grotto.

'I don't have a car.'

'Lucan says we can take his truck. He told me to get you all to drive it, see how you like it.'

So I shut Sweet William indoors, found my wallet and walked along the road with Princess to Cockerdoody's house.

'Catfish caught me a mud puppy over there in Morgan City. He brought it over here in a bucket. I took it into Cockerdoody's bedroom; he loves critters, so I showed him. It cheered him up, I believe, 'cept he called it a congo eel. Says he caught one like it in a ditch once outside of Stowell; says a nigger stole it and ate it chicken-fried. I never heard of no congo eel with a collar on it. Old Cockerdoody says some grow collars and some don't; it's the same with legs. I still reckon this one's a mud puppy.'

'What is it?' It sounded weird. 'Is it some kind of fish?'

'It ain't a fish if it got hands and feet. More like a lizard. You all never seen a mud puppy? Ooh boy.'

'Where is it?'

'I left it in Cockerdoody's yard. You all can take a look at it. Reckon I'll go ahead and turn it loose today.'

'Do they live in Texas? You should be careful.'

'Heck, it ain't *so* different here than in Louisiana. I never seen mud puppies round here. Still, I ain't never seen one anywhere much before. Only in pictures.'

I was very intrigued. When we got to the big green house, Princess fetched a large black fisherman's bucket, covered with a square of hardboard. Inside was a strange coiled slithy creature, like a greyish axolotl with blue spots, a spinal ridge and a red feathery ruff over its gills. Its head was blunt, with small bright eyes exuding – I thought – a cold malevolence towards its captors. The mud puppy was a little over a foot long.

Princess said, 'You all can pick him up – he don't sting.'

I didn't want to.

She said, 'I think he's radical. Real weird and freakish. We can set him free over by Horseshoe Lake.'

Catfish came to the door. I asked after his father. 'Just about the same.' He shrugged, implying that it was polite of me to ask but really none of my business, and he handed me Lucan's keys.

We got into the truck and I asked Princess about the Moody Gardens. 'Oh, they got a 3-D Imax theatre, you know it's six storeys high, and a Rainforest Pyramid.'

'Why Moody?'

'The Moody family paid for it.' That was rather a disappointment.

We stopped at the Horseshoe Liquor and Meat Mart so that she could buy a Big Red, then headed along Highway 87 to the crossroads. Princess was an excited passenger, sticking her head out of the window so that her hair came untied again and flared out like orange flames in the breeze.

'I got a joint from Lucilla – you all gonna smoke it with me?' But I was nervous in Lucan's truck, in case I would absent-mindedly drive on the wrong side of the road.

I stopped the truck near where Happy Jack and Ronny Sue had been fishing.

'Let's free the mud puppy now,' I said, eager to be rid of it.

Princess drank her Big Red (it smelt of bubblegum), then hurled the can into the water. She took the black bucket from the bed of the truck, walked to the edge of the water and tipped the mud puppy out.

For a couple of seconds I saw it clearly; it was like a huge newt. Entering the water, it tilted as if to display for us the iridescence of its skin, to show that it was a splendid creature in its element, its red collar a fabulous dandyish adornment. 'Oh wow,' muttered Princess as it swam out of sight. Later I found out it was a type of salamander (*Necturus maculosus*) but I never discovered if mud puppies exist west of the Sabine.

Princess said, 'I believe there's a toad in Hawaii you all can lick and get real high; like its skin is hallucinogenic. Ain't that bitchin'?'

A midge blew into my eye just as we joined the queue for the ferry. 'That's the reason for eyelashes, I believe,' mewed Princess and burst out laughing.

Once we were on the ferry she ran upstairs into the passenger lounge. I followed her. Leaning into the wind, her jutting chin made her look like a figurehead.

When we were back in the truck, I asked her when the baby was due. 'It's overdue,' she replied nonchalantly. The disclosure worried me: I could just see an emergency at the Moody Gardens.

We cruised along Broadway, past stately villas and flowering trees, listening to the Chris Ledoux tape and Princess asked if I knew what flowers were edible. 'You know, there's a whole bunch you *can* eat.' She told me that a schoolfriend of hers lived for a week on leaves and berries that he picked from parks and gardens on the island.

When we reached the beginning of Interstate 45 we turned down 81st Street, crossing Offatts Bayou, then headed right towards the airport. The Moody Gardens overlooked the bayou; there was a great glass pyramid and a big white building like a shopping mall. Inside was the Imax theatre, a vast cinema screen.

We lined up for tickets and were given red and green 3-D glasses.

The screen was massive: at least 120 feet high and 80 feet wide; you could only focus on parts of the image. The film was a documentary about a sculptor in Nevada; much of the footage was of the scenery and wildlife that inspired him and the three-dimensional effects were impressive. It reminded me of the short film they used to show in West End cinemas before the main feature . . . but as watched by a mouse. The audience, consisting mainly of old people, would gasp and shout 'Oh, my lord!' as giant jackrabbits seemed to jump out of the screen or the sculptor tipped molten iron from a bucket. Princess, sipping intermittently from a gigantic paper cup of Coca Cola, whispered: 'Regular movies would be better this big. Have you all seen the *Hellraiser* series? Movies like that should be Imax.'

We left the cinema and trooped around an exhibition about ecology before entering the glass pyramid. Inside the pleasure dome were all kinds of trees and plants, butterflies, birds, waterfalls, and ponds of ornamental fish. Princess told me that the pyramid was new so the trees were still quite small; eventually they would form a real rainforest with canopies and it would be more like a jungle than a greenhouse. She thought it was very exciting. She knew all about 'eco-spheres'. The same friend who had existed for a week on the flowers of Galveston was designing one of his own.

On our way back across town she asked me to stop again so that we could get some frozen yoghurt. We went to a stand in a mall on the Strand. There was a dark cross-eyed boy working behind the counter. Princess put on a breathy, romantic voice. 'That's my boyfriend, Karim. His parents are French, it's a French name. We're gettin' married soon.' Karim came around the counter and kissed her slowly on the mouth. He was wary of me and that made his squint worse. When Karim was serving some other people, I asked Princess if he was the father of her child. She shook her head. 'No. I've only known him a little while. I reckon he'll make a real good daddy. Karim the Dream. My baby's gonna have a real swarthy, fine-lookin' daddy. He could be French or Mexican.' It was a strange thing to say.

Karim told us that he was about to stop work for the day. Princess decided that she would wait for him so I left her at the frozen-yoghurt stand.

As I was walking back to where I had parked I met Monty Richardson, who said, 'That's a fine truck, brother.'

'It's not mine. I've borrowed it.'

Monty was on his way to the library. He was wearing a very tight sky-blue T-shirt and turquoise corduroy trousers; he was all flushed and sweaty. 'Tell me, which is the best novel by Sir Kingsley Amis?'

Just in time to spare me from what would have been a tedious digression, along came Henry Glover. He was in a terrible state, jabbering loudly as he drifted along. He was moving slowly as if weighed down by a great burden and he didn't recognize me.

'I personally am responsible for the highest of all mountains. OK, it was not growin' so I fixed it. It's made from white sugar.

There is no reason, no reason at all, why folks could not be housed there. Tourists would come, it would be remunerative.'

'Oh, boy. A fruitcake,' sneered Monty Richardson.

'Actually he's an artist. He's pretty talented. I've seen some of his pictures.'

'You're shitting me! What are you doing talking to trolls?'

'Hello, Henry. Did you get the job you went for?'

Something clicked and he recognized me. 'No, baby, no. It was a spiral, you know, an eddy.'

'What kind of job was it?' asked Monty.

'Short-term,' Henry Glover replied, regaining lucidity by the second.

'I guess there aren't many jobs going on the island. Don't know why people come here for work.'

'I come here to check the gallery situation. Disheartening, disheartening.'

'I got an aunt with a gallery,' Monty said. 'Show me the pictures and maybe I'll recommend you to her.'

I left the two of them arranging a viewing, fairly certain that Henry Glover would snap at any hand that offered to feed him, and I drove towards the ferry landing. For a while I listened to Chris Ledoux but rodeo songs quickly pall.

□ □

When I got back to Port Bolivar a big white Lexus, with gold-plated chrome, was parked outside Miss Kinsolver's trailer. Mary Alice, who had not seen the car pull up, was most intrigued. She sat on the deck, eager to find out who owned such an expensive vehicle. She told me it was the first time she had seen anyone visit Miss Kinsolver.

After a long wait we saw a middle-aged couple emerge from the trailer. The man stooped to pass through the door; he was tall and broad-shouldered, dressed in a belted safari jacket. The woman wore a lacy Victorian blouse with a high frilled collar and a skirt made of patchwork. The man turned back to Miss Kinsolver. 'Darlene, it was good to see you. Now, you call us any time.'

Mary Alice's face lit up and she clapped her hands with excitement. She leant over the railing of the deck and called out. 'Bart Studer! I'd know that voice anywhere!'

Bart Studer looked across to the House of Blue Lights. 'Holy moly! Mary Alice!'

Mary Alice ran, squealing, down the steps. Bart Studer was slightly shaken. 'This is one hell of a surprise. I don't think I seen you since the Gerald Ford campaign. Myrtle dear, um, this is Mary Alice . . . I don't recall your last name . . .'

'Oh, I just go by Mary Alice.'

Bart Studer adopted an exaggerated 'good old boy' manner, peppering his speech with cowboy slang. 'She helped us raise a whole passel of money up there in Dallas,' he drawled. 'We had us enough to burn a wet mule that night.'

Myrtle smiled condescendingly. Mary Alice touched her arm. 'Shoot. All I did was jump out of a big old cake. Now, tell me what brings y'all to the peninsula.'

'Darlene Kinsolver is my husband's cousin. If ever we come down to the coast we like to check on her. You know she has a nervous disorder.'

'I know she suffers,' replied Mary Alice briskly. She stood back and looked Myrtle Studer up and down. 'Why, that is the prettiest get-up! That skirt reminds me of a pieced quilt!'

'Baby, it *was* a pieced quilt. Cost me an arm and leg in that damn Galleria,' declared Bart Studer. 'Myrtle likes everything to be old-fashioned, everything. You should see the antique furniture we had shipped over from England.'

'I got a lodger from England. Joseph, you come down and meet the Studers from Dallas! This is Joseph; he's fixin' to write a book.'

Myrtle Studer, glad to talk to anyone other than a middle-aged Popsy, told me, 'I love England. It is my spiritual home. I can appreciate the lifestyle, you see. Some Americans can't – many are real ignorant. It depends on their family background, I guess.' She glanced over at the House of Blue Lights. Two cats were copulating in full view. 'I hope you are not getting the wrong impression of our country. It's kind of backward down here.'

'Oh hush, it's so peaceful,' Mary Alice scolded her, tossing her hair with a spritely movement and smiling at Bart Studer. Myrtle sighed, as if at her husband's weak-mindedness. She wanted to talk about books.

'Do you know the novels of Monica Dickens? She's just as great as her ancestor Charles. I have first editions sent directly to me by my friend, the Baroness Temple. Whenever she finds one, she sends it over to me. Some of them have that gold blocking. Do you know the Baroness? She runs a book-search business out of Chelt-en-ham in the Cotswold hills.'

Bart Studer told me that their daughter was named Elizabeth, 'after your Queen over there'. He asked me if I liked steak. 'Then you are a lucky man. I got a box of six rib-eyes in the trunk there. Seems like old Darlene don't want 'em. Man, that's damn good USDA prime aged beef. Sent to me from Scottsdale, Arizona. Gourmet Club of Arizona. All vacuum-packed but she won't touch it. You can have 'em.'

'It's very kind of you. Are you sure you wouldn't rather take them home?'

'Joseph, we got us an entire cow in our freezer.' Myrtle pulled a long-suffering expression.

Bart laughed. 'She ain't kiddin' either.'

After the Studers had gone, Mary Alice opened a pint of schnapps; she seemed wistful. I asked what the matter was.

She told me that Bart Studer had been her sugarman for a while during her dancing days. 'I just hate for him to see me old and fat like this.'

'You're much prettier than his wife,' I told her.

She laughed. 'Baby, I know that's true. That skirt was so deeky.'

Mary Alice was mercurial when drunk; she could plunge from squealing gaiety to lachrymose torpor in the space of two swigs. I could tell that she was presently inclined to sadness; her lip had already started trembling. She spoke and acted just like an unhappy fifteen-year-old.

'That old Myrtle took one look at me and decided I was a tramp.'

'Don't worry about her.'

'No, baby, I don't. Just sometimes I get hurt by things people call me.'

'You're very popular on the peninsula,' I told her.

'Well, I know that's true. Down here they don't judge too hard.'

'So what does it matter what one woman thinks?'

'It ain't one woman, Joseph, I got a *bad* reputation. I got to face it. That's hard on a woman. Baby, I been labelled a tramp by a judge and jury.' The tears began to roll. 'I been called a drunken whore and an unfit mother . . .'

'I didn't know you were a mother.'

Mary Alice was outraged and further wounded by my ignorance. 'I am too! Might even be a grandmother! Natalie's gonna be twenty-eight this fall.'

'Where is she?'

'She won't have nothin' to do with me. I asked for custody of her back when I had some money. Herm fought me through the courts. I lost bad, Joseph. They weren't about to approve of my lifestyle, now were they? Herm was more conventional in their eyes. Worse part was Natalie got scared of me . . . everybody sayin' I'm a lowdown hooker . . . her own mother, Joseph . . . Herm's wicked lies . . . I ain't even seen her for fifteen years.' For the next ten minutes she lay on her bed crying.

I asked what we were going to do with the steaks. We could share them with Catfish and Lucan. Mary Alice wasn't hungry; she said that Lucilla would keep them in her refrigerator for us.

Then Lucilla showed up with some croissant-like pastries she called 'butterhorns'. She hugged Mary Alice and told her that she was 'a fine good-natured lady and a credit to the peninsula', which cheered her up a lot.

Lucilla had been talking to a telephone clairvoyant from La Toya Jackson's Psychic Network. It was a service that operated from Boca Raton in Florida, dispensing mystical advice on matters of love, health and money at $3.99 a minute.

I had come to realize that, in the absence of organized religion, soothsayers and faith-healers of varying authenticity met the spiritual needs of these women. It would have been pointless to suggest they were wasting their money when they so clearly benefited from the service. Furthermore, the organized religion that was generally offered was intolerant and paranoid, railing against social progress; Lucilla, with her telephone psychics, and Mary Alice, with her Love Soap and Van Van Oil, were kinder and more compassionate than any Born-Again zealots. But I was intrigued by this particular transaction. 'Do you actually speak to La Toya?'

'No, you talk to the same psychics that she talks to, that's all; I guess she lets them use her name,' Lucilla told me, slightly defensively. The clairvoyant had advised her to leave Texas, to move nearer her sister in Slidell.

I suggested that she move to New Orleans.

'I wish!' exclaimed Lucilla. She was fascinated by anything magical or Gothic (her favourite novelists were Anne Rice and Virginia Andrews) and she told me that New Orleans was the psychic centre of America.

□ □

The next morning, at Pirate's Cove, Lucan was fuming.

A dancer with the bizarre name of Ultima had arrived at Cockerdoody's house at four in the morning, looking for him. She worked at his clubs in Sulphur. Lucan was angry that Ultima had followed him to Texas because she was an addict, specializing in pharmaceuticals (Dilaudid, Demerol) and not averse to holding up the drugstores of towns she passed through.

'The chick is a friggin' pain,' he told me, 'nothin' but trouble. Those green-and-whites will be down here too, if she's as crazy as she's actin'.'

I asked why she had come all this way.

'I *guess* I owe her some wages. That's what she claims. It ain't that far to come. She'll be gone by noon.' He took a swig of Schlitz

Malt Liquor, wiping his mouth on the back of his hand.

Minutes later Ultima burst into the coffee lounge. She was a frightening maniacal creature, a dark frizzy-haired wraith in a green lycra leotard, with black nails and clown's make-up. Her age was impossible to determine. She wasn't exactly ugly – she looked wild and double-jointed like a woman painted by Egon Schiele.

'Why dincha wake me? Do ya think I wanna be cooped in with a dyin' man? What the hell, Lucan. Ya don't think of others! That is your trouble.'

The voice was like an oboe played by an untalented child, a spittly cross between a shriek and a sob. Ultima scurried about the lounge in little spidery bursts of fury.

I drank my coffee and read about a baby girl in Leesburg, Florida, born with two functional hearts.

'Three hundred bucks and now, buster.'

'Ultima, Ultima. Will you just chill!'

'Yeah? Well, fuck you, buddy! Three hundred bucks and I need it.'

'I told you, spelled it out for you. We go to Galveston and we make a cash withdrawal on Mastercard. Then you get back in your car and out of the goddamn state!' Lucan kept pulling at his purple cowboy shirt and he crunched the empty can in his fist. 'Jesus, girl. That is my uncle coughin' himself to death back there. I have that on my mind without your crap.'

'Yeah, yeah, yeah,' whined Ultima.

At the edge of the marsh was a dancing man, or a man who had lost control of his limbs in some frightful chorea. He was thrashing about on the border of dry land between the side of Loop 108 and the water. It was Happy Jack.

He looked like somebody being electrocuted. His face was contorted into a grimace like a Greek mask: a wide open mouth curving upwards into a gaping smile and eyes rolled back. I hurried over to him.

As soon as Happy Jack saw me coming, he pulled himself together. His face straightened and he regained his composure. I asked if he was all right.

'Excellent, man. Everything is excellent.'

He still looked shaky and far from well.

'Do you want to come in?' I asked, indicating the House of Blue Lights.

'No, dude. Thank you. This is where I wanna be. This is excellent.'

I walked on towards the house and, as I was climbing the stairs, I looked back and saw that Happy Jack had started to twitch again, but perhaps less wildly.

Later in the day I mentioned his odd behaviour to Mary Alice. She told me she wasn't surprised. 'That poor kid has so many problems.'

Suddenly I felt alienated, incapable of making sense of what was going on around me. I could understand books but not real events; that was the condition of being an outsider. I felt adrift, miles away from everything.

To make things worse Mary Alice was drunk again so any conversation was hit-and-miss.

She had met, and been horrified by, Ultima. Mary Alice was astonished by her lack of charm. To her, strippers were showgirls, akin to beauty queens and cheerleaders, wholesome sirens whose *raison d'être* was to be prettier than ordinary women, certainly prettier than the sugarmen's wives.

'People in Louisiana pay to watch *that* girl dance? Boy, those coonasses! Ultimate – what kinda name is that? Just about as ugly as she is. That Ultimate girl should be paid to keep her clothes on!'

'Mary Alice,' I said, 'with no disrespect to Lucan, those clubs are bound to be sleazy places. I bet most of the girls have drug problems.'

Sometimes, particularly when she was in an emotional state, she would speak to me as if I were a child. 'Now, Joseph, y'all promise me not to take drugs. They are the devil's curse. You just promise now.'

□ □

Lucilla brought me a pile of books about voodoo. One or two were quite scholarly; most of them were lurid and sensational. To be honest, I preferred the lurid ones. Lucilla laughed and said that she did too. She told me that her sister in Slidell worked in an old-folks' home and one of her very oldest charges, the 103-year-old Miss Howard, was rumoured to be the daughter of Prince Basile. I was not familiar with the prince so Lucilla opened various books at the relevant passages. 'I guess he wasn't no top flight Voodoo but what you can gather makes kind of a neat story. I reckon they could make a movie.'

Prince Basile, whose real name was Joseph Howard, was a quadroon (three quarters white) from Gretna, just across the Mississippi from New Orleans, who regularly attended the rituals presided over by the Voodoo Queen, Marie Laveau; they were strange bacchanalian events.

The celebrants, male and female, undressed, either completely or to their undergarments. Marie Laveau remained fully clothed. She wore a long blue robe, and around her head was tied a *tignon* with seven protruding knots; she wore large gold hoop earrings and gold bracelets; when the weather was cool, she wore a plaid stole that she claimed was a present from Queen Victoria.

A large white sheet was spread on the ground; candles, of various colours, were lit around its edges; in the middle were five empty bottles. The celebrants brought bottles of rum and tafia and, as soon the ritual commenced, there was drumming and dancing; the liquor was ceremonially sprinkled on the sheet and over each other. Marie Laveau, standing among the empty bottles in the very centre of the sheet, called out instructions to the dancers, as if at a square dance. Intermittently she took a mouthful of tafia and blew it into the face of one of the celebrants. All the while there would be rapturous chanting.

In the middle of the ritual Marie Laveau would bring out a huge python, a docile 20-foot-long creature called Zombi, that was transported in a big palmetto basket. She would wrap the snake about herself and perform a writhing, twisting dance, her feet never leaving the ground.

After the snake was produced, the celebrants became more frenzied, the dancing faster and faster.

People collapsed with exhaustion, others disported themselves with sexual abandon, and Marie Laveau's eyes would roll back until only the whites showed.

Robert Tallant, in *Voodoo in New Orleans*, calls Prince Basile a witch doctor, but he seems to have attracted women followers with pure sexual magnetism rather than any more esoteric powers. He was a most energetic and erotic dancer.

Marie Laveau, with her instinct for crowd-pulling, encouraged him to participate in the ceremonies, and it was she who invented his royal designation. Prince Basile's ceremonial role was to take the place of the python after Zombi died of mouth rot.

A cauldron of boiling water would be placed in the middle of the ceremonial space and into it would be tossed magical herbs, coloured powders and sometimes live chickens.

Marie Laveau would announce '*L'Appé vini, le Grand Zombi!*' and Prince Basile would spring from the darkness beyond the candle-light, landing right in front of the Voodoo Queen. He would be wearing very few clothes, and carrying a baby's coffin that was placed at Marie Laveau's feet. Prince Basile then began a wild, whirling dance. The celebrants chanted, '*Le Grand Zombi! Le Grand Zombi!*' When his dance was over, the brew in the cauldron would be ready to drink.

Prince Basile, who lived in a hut, not far from the Voodoo Queen's, beside the Bayou St John, figures in a horrid, somewhat operatic story:

Euphrasine Tabouis was the only child of a jeweller. She grew up, above his shop, in Royal Street. Her mother had died giving birth.

Tabouis adored his daughter. He bought her the best clothes that he could afford, and sent her to be educated at the Ursuline Convent; his great wish was that she would marry into one of the grand Creole families. Often, when she was a little girl, he would daydream aloud about her wedding.

Many of Euphrasine's schoolfriends at the Convent were the daughters of grandees and she would be invited to play at the great houses of the Vieux Carré. She was a pretty girl; the jeweller was often complimented on her charm and the ease with which she moved in smart society.

Tabouis's ambition seemed within reach, and he spent all his profits buying Euphrasine the accoutrements she needed to fit into the world he had groomed her for.

When Euphrasine was fourteen, Tabouis suddenly fell ill; his doctor informed him that he had a blood infection and, at the longest, two months to live.

Tabouis had very little money to leave Euphrasine, for he had spent it all at the dressmaker's, and they had no relatives in New Orleans; he worried that the dream would be dashed by his death.

Euphrasine was too young to be married. It would not do to appeal to the parents of her friends. Tabouis attempted to sell the jewellery shop but there were no takers; all the while he grew weaker and weaker.

One day, when Tabouis could barely stand, a Parisian, recently arrived in New Orleans, came to look at the business.

The Frenchman's name was Jules Pigeon; although he was by no means handsome, Tabouis detected a certain refinement in his manners and an elegance of dress. In despair, he made Pigeon a proposal. Pigeon could have the shop for nothing, so long as he promised to look after Euphrasine.

Tabouis made the terms of the agreement clear: part of the money that Pigeon would save by not having to pay for the business would go towards keeping Euphrasine in the manner she was accustomed to. Pigeon agreed, and presently Tabouis died.

Euphrasine Tabouis detested Jules Pigeon at first sight. The name, she thought, suited him, for his appearance was revoltingly columbine: his eyes were round and practically lashless; his mouth was tiny and the upper lip covered the lower; his head was smaller than his long white neck, and his shoulders were narrower than his hips.

Pigeon's reaction to Euphrasine was quite the opposite; he seethed with desire for the Creole maiden. Sometimes he sat up late at night drinking absinthe, until his craving became so fierce that he would enter her bedroom, to molest her while she slept. Euphrasine would wake up and struggle with Pigeon, whose drunken lechery terrified her. The next morning Pigeon would bring her flowers, or a new bonnet, but still Euphrasine despised him.

After her father's death, and as her unconventional arrangements became known, Euphrasine was invited to the grand houses less regularly. To begin with, Pigeon, who was considerably less worldly and *soigné* than Tabouis had supposed, would insist upon chaperoning his ward, and he could not hold his liquor; he was unacceptable. Euphrasine let her schoolfriends know how much she hated her guardian. The outcome was that she lost the little respect she had earned.

Creole gentlemen customarily kept mistresses. Euphrasine Tabouis, as her social standing collapsed, received many generous proposals. To escape the vile attentions of Pigeon, she began to slip away, to the private rooms of restaurants or the *loges grillées* at the Opera House, where she was entertained by the brothers and fathers of her former classmates. She would return home drunk, if she returned at all, and, after the ensuing row, Pigeon would be the more tearful.

One St John's Eve Euphrasine went with a party of revellers to the voodoo ceremony on the banks of the Pontchartrain.

Throughout the ritual she could not take her eyes off Prince Basile; although he was shorter than she was, he was simply the most attractive man she had ever seen. It was a hot night and the dancer wore only a pair of red satin breeches, a bracelet of silver bells on his left ankle, and sapphire earrings.

His skin was not black, nor was it between colours; it was a unique burnished golden shade that she had never seen before. Euphrasine thought it was a complexion to grace an antique god. His loose curls were of shining copper.

Prince Basile's eyes were the brightest green, transmitting a light that Euphrasine found hard and frightening; they were barely human; they made the humanity of others look like weakness.

Afterwards Euphrasine disappeared. The revellers, who were mostly drunk, returned to town without her. Pigeon notified the police. When the trail led to Marie Laveau, the police withdrew. They were intimidated by her powers.

Pigeon was informed that, in all likelihood, Euphrasine had fallen into the bayou and drowned. He walked up and down Royal Street all afternoon howling, his little head thrown back; then he tried to poison himself, unsuccessfully.

Euphrasine had, of course, run off with Prince Basile. The hut he took her to was furnished only with a bed and that was no more than a pile of ragged quilts. By all accounts, he was a type of sadist who enjoyed scratching and cutting his lovers with blades and broken glass. Neighbours and passers-by often heard screams and groans.

Euphrasine stayed with the dancer for an entire year.

The following St John's Eve, Prince Basile brought home another woman, jet-black and over six foot tall, who, while Prince Basile stood and laughed, chased the wretched, exhausted Euphrasine out of the hut and into the woods. There she collapsed and was, for days, unconscious.

She was found by an Englishman, a retired schoolmaster called Arthur Egerton-Clough who habitually wandered the woods at night and who, upon discovering that the eighteen-year-old girl was without funds or family, delivered her to a brothel.

This wasn't such a dreadful fate. The bagnio Euphrasine Tabouis found herself in was a luxurious one. The clients were received in elegant drawing-rooms, full of walnut and mahogany furniture. Her boudoir was sumptuous. The dresses provided were even finer and more expensive than those that her father had bought her, and she was allowed to keep the presents of money and jewellery that her clients (many of them, again, the brothers and fathers of her schoolfriends) gave her.

Euphrasine seemed happy enough in her new position; she had a certain security and success; the unexpected ferocity of her love-making made her by far the most sought-after girl in the house.

One summer evening she persuaded an elderly admirer to lend her his carriage. She put on her finest dress and jewels, and instructed the coachman to take her to the woods, where the Bayou St John enters the Pontchartrain.

Prince Basile was alone that evening, and delighted to entertain his former lover. All night long they fought like cats.

In the morning, bruised and bleeding, no doubt afraid that her career might be in jeopardy, Euphrasine said something that offended the voodoo dancer. He took a cane-cutter's machete, held it high in the air so that the sun caught the blade, and brought it down slowly across her left foot.

Somehow, three days later, Euphrasine arrived at the jewellery shop in Royal Street. Pigeon, having accepted that she was dead, was elated. He carried her upstairs and bathed her and he sent for a doctor to examine her gashed foot.

The doctor saw that the metatarsal tendons were severed. Euphrasine would be crippled for the rest of her life, and reliant upon the man she despised.

One night, soon after her return, Pigeon woke her up. He was naked. Euphrasine burst out laughing. The laughter was ugly and terrible, as loud as a scream, and shrill with insanity. It went on for hours.

The neighbours sent for the police, but by the time they arrived Euphrasine was silent again.

She never left the apartment above the shop until Pigeon died in 1921. Then, for at least twenty years, she was an ancient, crippled beggar (people believed that she was a hundred years old) crouched outside the Café du Monde.

Lucilla's film of the story would star Julia Roberts as Euphrasine, Prince as Prince Basile and 'probably that English actor played Hannibal Lector' as Pigeon.

I was getting concerned about my accommodation in New Orleans. In her letter my friend had told me she would arrange for me to sublet a neighbour's apartment. It was impossible to get in touch with her. I knew that Mary Alice's stepbrother Repton lived in New Orleans so I asked her if he might know of a sublet.

Mary Alice sighed. 'Honey, he's so fragile now. I don't like to burden him with anything. Oh, I know he'd want to help y'all; it's just he can't hardly walk any more and he's gettin' worse every year.'

What was the matter with him?

'Joseph, it is just the saddest story. He was hit by a ricochetin' bullet. Back in the Howard Johnson shoot-out.'

I knew a bit about the shoot-out, which had taken place in January 1973. It seemed to have happened longer than twenty years ago and the existence of survivors, for some reason, sounded unlikely. This was because my knowledge of the incident originated from a song. It was as if somebody had said, 'I was in *that* riot in Cell Block Number Nine.'

The facts are straightforward. In June 1972, Mark Essex arrived in New Orleans from Emporia, Kansas. He had told his parents that he was going south to 'learn to live like a black man'.

He was twenty-three years old; his adult life had so far been troubled.

Essex came from a middle-class family and had graduated from high school before enlisting in the navy. Expecting to serve in Vietnam, he never left the United States. His naval training provided his first experience of outright racial discrimination and harassment. High-school contemporaries who remembered Mark Essex as a relaxed, cheerful sort were surprised at the cagey, embittered young man who returned on leave. At his base in San Diego, Essex was involved in numerous altercations with white sailors. His closest friend in the navy was a man called Rodney Frank, a militant black from New Orleans, who introduced him to the concept of Black Power and taught him about the Black Panthers and the Black Muslims.

In January 1971 Essex showed up in Emporia, absent without leave. His parents persuaded him to return to California to face a court martial. Essex was given a dishonorable discharge based on a 'character behavior disorder'.

He then crossed the country to New York City, where for several months he worked as a volunteer at the Black Panther headquarters.

Later that year Mark Essex moved back to live with his parents, but he could not find work in Kansas and he argued continually with his father. By the following summer everyone had had enough of the situation; Mark Essex decided to join his friend Rodney Frank in New Orleans.

The move failed to provide the direction. Essex found that the New Orleans Black Panthers were neither as organized nor as dynamic as those in New York. Rodney Frank had, by this time, converted to Islam and his interests were more spiritual than political; while Essex was sympathetic to the Black Muslims, he was not convinced. By and large he considered the black community in New Orleans politically lethargic, and he found himself an angry, isolated man. He moved into an apartment at 2619 Dryades Street and enrolled in a government-sponsored training programme, learning how to repair vending machines.

Two events that year affected him deeply.

The first was the formation of the Felony Action Squad by Clarence Giarusso, Superintendent of the New Orleans Police Department, in September. A self-regulated élite force whose mission was to patrol the high crime areas of the city (invariably the black housing projects known as 'the bricks'), the Felony Action Squad had a policy of shooting to kill if confronted with trouble. The black community were outraged by what they saw as racist policing and tried in various ways, unsuccessfully, to have the squad disbanded.

The second, which happened on 16 November, was the shooting by the police of two black student leaders, Leonard Brown and Denver Smith, at Southern University in Baton Rouge. Other militant students were either arrested or banned from campus. No legal action was taken against the sheriff's deputies, despite protests.

Mark Essex brooded, and sometimes he talked to the Panthers. For six weeks he tried to organize some retaliatory action but in vain. Eventually, on New Year's Eve, he wrote a letter to the WWL television station:

> Africa greets you. On December 31, 1972 appt 11 the Downtown N.O. Police Dept. will be attack. Reason = many. But the death of two innocent brothers will be avenged. And many others. P.S. Tell Pig Gurusso the felony action squad aint shit. MATA.

The letter was not addressed to anyone in particular and was not opened for a couple of weeks.

At 10.45 that night, Essex stationed himself in a field opposite the Central Lock-Up with a .44-calibre deer rifle.

He took aim at a police officer driving up to the building. The bullet missed the target but a second bullet hit a black cadet, Alfred Harrell, who had run to help the officer. Harrell died instantly.

An hour later the police answered a burglar-alarm call in a warehouse on South Lopez Street. An officer called Edwin Hosli entered the building to investigate and was met by sniper fire.

Hosli fired back and grazed Essex's hand; then he collapsed, while Essex escaped, and he died that night in hospital.

On New Year's Day 1973 there was a house-to-house search of the area, called Gert Town, around the warehouse.

The policemen who conducted the search were upset at losing two of their number and angry that the (mainly black) residents proved unhelpful. Resentment flared on both sides, and Superintendent Giarusso decided to call off the investigation to allow things to cool down. He also requested that the media keep silent, to avoid racial unrest.

That evening, at half past six, the police received a call from the Revd Sylvester Williams, who had discovered a young man hiding in the First New St Mark's Baptist Church at 1208 South Lopez. Essex, still unidentified, had vanished by the time the police arrived, but they found blood stains and evidence of his having slept there.

The following evening, Tuesday, 2 January, Essex went into Joe's Grocery, at 4200 Erato Street, to buy a razor and some blades. The proprietor, Joe Pernicaro, noticed that the young man, who was acting nervously, had a loosely bandaged hand that he kept tucked into the pocket of his jacket, and that the bandage was blood-stained.

After serving Essex, he rang the police and told them that he was convinced that the young man was the sniper who had killed Officer Hosli.

On Wednesday evening an unidentified woman called the police to report a young man breaking into the same Baptist church on South Lopez.

Again the police arrived too late: all they found was a note addressed to the pastor, apologizing for breaking the lock, and stating the intention 'to get right with the Lord'.

On Sunday, 7 January, at half past ten in the morning, Mark Essex entered Joe's Grocery again. This time he was carrying a rifle.

'You're the one!' he shouted to Joe Pernicaro, and fired straight into the grocer's chest.

Pernicaro lived just long enough to identify his assailant as the same young man he had reported on Tuesday.

Minutes later Marvin Albert told the police that an armed man had stolen his car; and immediately after that Tamar Friedman reported to police that a hit-and-run vehicle had damaged her car, its number plate that of Albert's car.

Police tracked the vehicle for a while, then lost it.

Mark Essex drove the stolen car to the multi-storey car park of the Howard Johnson's Motor Lodge on Loyola Avenue, abandoning it at the fourth level. His reckless driving drew attention and soon the police realized that they had found the sniper.

A gun battle followed that lasted until the evening. Essex, who seems to have fired at random, killed nine people and injured thirteen.

Police and armed civilians returned fire; bullets ricocheted off the walls and wounded more people. Mary Alice's stepbrother Repton was one of the wounded; she did not think he had been armed. 'He just won't talk about it anyhow.'

At 8.15 Essex emerged on the roof of the Motor Lodge. A barrage of gunfire pumped 200 bullets into his twitching body.

The police, convinced that Essex had accomplices, continued firing all night.

It was not until the evening of the next day that the incident was officially declared over.

Detectives searching Essex's apartment at 2619 Dryades Street found political graffiti on the walls, as well as evidence that he had been studying Swahili; Mata, the name that Essex had used in his warning letter, means 'the bow' in Swahili. His flight to the Howard Johnson car park appears to have been premeditated: a map was found with the building circled.

The funeral of Mark Essex was held in Emporia, Kansas, and attended by several national representatives of the Black Panthers.

A speaker at the graveside announced, 'He will never really die as long as the will to struggle is alive in the hearts and minds of Black America.'

In 1981, on the album *Reflections*, Gil Scott-Heron recorded a version of Marvin Gaye's 'Inner City Blues'. That is where I first heard about Mark Essex, for Scott-Heron inserted a verse about the shoot-out.

Repton had been working as a chef at the time he was shot. Now he worked part-time at the Tulane University library. Mary Alice offered me his address anyway and encouraged me to contact him when I got to New Orleans.

I was on such a tight budget that I didn't want to stay in motels if I could help it. I wished I knew more people in New Orleans. I took Repton's address, in case he knew of anyone who planned to be out of town for a month or two.

Eight

LATER THE NEXT WEEK COCKERDOODY DIED. IT HAPPENED IN THE MIDDLE OF the night. I heard the news the following morning (it was a Saturday) in the coffee lounge. 'There's gone be a party tonight – that was what he wanted.'

I went back to the House of Blue Lights and played the jukebox. I liked to choose about twenty songs, then sit outside writing letters. Ray Charles was singing 'That Lucky Old Sun' when Mary Alice returned from the Homestead.

She was very tired. 'Ooh, honey! My dogs are barkin'!' she announced.

She told me she had heard about the death, within an hour of its occurrence, from one of her customers. 'All those shrimpers are tight like that; word gets around.' She insisted that I accompany her to the party. I felt that I would be intruding. 'No, baby. Y'all know Catfish and Lucan.'

Sometimes Mary Alice would spread a sheet of black oilskin on the floor and assemble a jigsaw puzzle from her collection. The puzzles she preferred had thousands of tiny pieces and could take as long as a week to complete. She worked from the corners inwards. When she concentrated, you could see the tip of her tongue at the side of her mouth.

I was never a jigsaw enthusiast. Mary Alice tried to explain their appeal. 'See, it don't matter how many times y'all have done it, still takes just as long. They ain't got no short cuts; it takes patience. Some people enjoy housework, tidyin' the place, gettin' things straight – it's kinda like the pleasure I get from jigsaws.'

She didn't enjoy housework at all.

The jigsaws were an attempt to make order from chaos, where neither the order nor the chaos encroached upon her life, for Mary Alice had an almost Taoist respect for disorderly fate; her life was a stream meandering through a forest where the trees kept falling down.

The pictures were displayed on the box lids. Mary Alice's favourite was Van Gogh's *The Starry Night*. Like many Americans, she pronounced the painter's name *Van Go*. She had embarked upon *The Starry Night* the previous afternoon.

Sweet William gave a querulous bark: somebody was coming up the steps. It was Miss Kinsolver, wearing a straw bonnet and a long ragged frock, like a costume from a pageant.

She was as pale as before; ashen, as if covered by a layer of dust. The powdery appearance made me wonder if Miss Kinsolver, for some reason, pretended to be much older than she was. People spoke of her as an old woman, which seemed odd because she was certainly younger than Mary Alice. Mary Alice was surprised to see her neighbour at the screen door.

'Why, Miss Kinsolver! Y'all just come on in. We ain't got no coffee but there's some Dr Pepper somewhere. You know my lodger, Joseph? He's over here from England.'

Miss Kinsolver would not come in. She stood at the door and swayed a little. Sweet William snarled at her from under the bed. When she spoke, clearly but very softly, it was in the strained tones of an invalid. 'There has been a death, hasn't there?'

'Yes, honey. Old Cockerdoody. You know how ill he's been.'

'There will be others,' announced Miss Kinsolver gravely.

'Now, girl. That's no way to talk.'

'There are bacilli in the water. It's poisoned water, filthy water, full of bacilli.'

'Well, I never do drink what comes out of the faucet, except to clean my teeth, but I sure ain't tasted no basil eye. Unless the toothpaste would drown the flavour, y'all reckon?'

Miss Kinsolver had turned around and was going down the steps.

Mary Alice scratched her head. 'Hoo whee.'

The visit had put her off the puzzle. She slept for the next five or six hours. When she woke up at half past four, she called out. 'Joseph, you wouldn't be headin' towards the store, by any chance?'

'I could go there; do you need something?'

I noticed an uncharacteristic shrillness of tone, some urgency. 'Baby, please get me some malt liquor, Olde English – you know the big bottle?'

□ □

About a hundred people had already gathered when Mary Alice and I arrived at the big green house at six. There were many old people, and several shrimpers wearing the short white wellington boots that shrimpers wear, and a few men in business suits, looking rather out of place.

There were three black cowboys. Many Texans, of course, wear Western clothes – it does not mean that they work on ranches; however, listening to the men's conversation, I could tell that they were genuine. They were from the King Ranch near Victoria.

Nowadays black cowboys may seem exotic (even comic, as in *Blazing Saddles*) because there is so much cowboy mythology that is exclusively white, but once they were the majority.

•

The American settlers moving west across the Sabine River into the Republic of Texas often found themselves in possession of larger tracts of land than they had owned within the United States. Cattle-ranching offered a more efficient and immediate use of the land than cultivation. The slaves the Americans brought with them, who would have been field-hands in states such as Mississippi, were transformed into cowboys, taught the necessary skills by Mexican *vaqueros*.

Some ranchers settled near the Rio Grande, but here they found that it was too easy for their slaves to escape – across the river into Mexico, where they were free. Throughout the ten years of the republic, and the twenty years of statehood before emancipation, these escapes into Mexico were common; slaves on horseback could move quickly.

East of the Nueces River, most slaves found it harder to escape; so there they stayed, in the bleak, rough country, herding wild cattle through the heavy coastal bush. Cattle crews throughout central and eastern Texas generally consisted of slave-cowboys.

There were even a few free blacks with their own ranches before the Civil War: Aaron Ashworth owned 2,500 cattle, as well as a crew of slaves to work them, and employed a white schoolmaster to tutor his children.

After the Civil War, black cowboys were free men with highly specialized skills. Employment was plentiful, blacks and whites working together, though few black cowboys became foremen or trail bosses.

The war itself had wreaked havoc upon the cattle business. For more than four years the cattle had roamed unattended and were scattered across the plains. They lurked in the brush and hid in the gullies and canyons. Calves had become wild cows and longhorned bulls, unbranded and unclaimed. It was the cowboy's job to capture them.

A well-known black cowboy from that era was Coyote Beckwith, who ventured into the densest thickets, working long hours alone, finding and branding the cattle.

Coyote Beckwith rode at night; he carried a gun and a machete, various lengths of rope, a bag of water, a bag of hard biscuits, and strips of pemmican. He eschewed alcohol but drank a vile brew of coffee mixed with chillies and wild herbs that enabled him to go without sleep for days on end.

Coyote Beckwith brought back hundreds of cows and bulls. Other cowboys were rounding up cattle in similar quantities. Texas now had at its disposal more cattle than its few markets demanded.

Factories were set up on the Brazos River. Herds of longhorn cattle were driven to these factories to be slaughtered. The hides became leather, the fat was used for soap and tallow; but the meat was thrown into the river, since there was so much more than the locals could eat. Catfish fed on the carcasses and grew to monstrous proportions. Sharks began to swim upriver from the Gulf of Mexico. All this was wasteful and unprofitable at a time when Americans were consuming more beef than ever before.

Texas had the beef but it was thousands of miles away from the markets; this necessarily led to the establishment of the cattle drive. Cattle could be herded across country to the great markets in Kansas, Nebraska and Colorado, which were linked to the populous eastern states by rail.

The Chisholm Trail, the Western Trail and the Goodnight-Loving Trail; the cattle drives brought the romantic image of the cowboy to the popular imagination.

Although to begin with there were many black cowboys, they were in time outnumbered by whites, and the lonesome cowboy of song and story was invariably white.

Most years, in Beaumont, there is an event called The Bill Pickett Invitational Rodeo after a famous black cowboy and rodeo star who invented the sport called 'bulldogging' – wrestling a steer to the ground. Pickett, who died in 1932, was a very great celebrity. He performed across the West and in Mexico City, in New York at Madison Square Garden. In London in 1914 Bill Pickett rode and roped and bulldogged before King George and Queen Mary.

Mary Alice and I were standing near the black cowboys. One of the three was an old man with white hair. Mary Alice smiled graciously. 'Good evening, Mr Lincoln.'

Mr Lincoln raised his hat to Mary Alice with a stern expression and murmured something about locusts and honey, then went straight back into his conversation with his friends across the trestle table. He spoke in a high nasal twang that I could barely comprehend; it was not unlike Bob Dylan's singing voice.

I have a friend whose grandfather was a famous cattleman. I asked if Mr Lincoln had ever worked on his ranch. He had, I think, in 1962. He clearly did not like the look or sound of me because that was as far as our conversation went.

Chairs and sofas had been brought out of the house and positioned around the yard. Three ice-chests were stuck with bright bottles and there were towers of disposable cups and plates. There was a keg of Budweiser.

Around the edges of the yard grew vibrant four o'clocks, and off to one side stood a rain tree (a sort of mimosa) covered with sweet-smelling bright-red flowers; the ground beneath it was sticky with a spittle secreted, Catfish explained, by cicadas. That seemed disgusting to me.

Two long trestle tables were draped with sheets of newspaper, on top of which were placed dishes of food.

The catering was supervised by Lucilla; most of the guests brought food and drink with them and Lucilla would issue instructions. She had provided an enormous Hamburger Corn Pie herself, as well as a Jell-O Shrimp Salad. 'We puttin' all the savoury things down this end, salads over there.'

There was a great pot of Dirty Rice, and mounds of boiled crawfish, and *boudin* sausages and various potato salads, dishes of red beans; and there were plates of cold fried chicken and fried frogs' legs, like double chicken drumsticks, much bigger than the frogs' legs in France, for the bullfrog of Texas and Louisiana (*rana catesbiana*) is an altogether heftier creature.

In the centre of one of the tables was a plate of Moon Pies and

Goo Goo Clusters – Cockerdoody's favourite candies – that nobody touched; I wondered if they were symbolic in some way.

Mr Advani arrived with two cardboard boxes: inside were countless bags of Fritos. 'Everybody loves Fritos,' he told me.

Many people brought raw meat for the barbecue pit. My contribution was the meat that Bart Studer had given me.

There was a distant growling that grew louder and closer. Six dragonish Harley Davidsons pulled up at Cockerdoody's house. The riders looked like medieval brigands; one had blue tears tattooed beneath his eyes; another, a Chicano, had a horrid plait, like a length of rope dipped in oil, about a yard long, that left streaks of brown grease all over the back of his denim waistcoat. A black pit-bull-terrier reclined on the gas tank of one of the bikes. Catfish greeted the Bandidos with a special handshake. The one with the tears was evidently the leader and his name was Donkey George.

Donkey George produced a gallon tub of Bluebell vanilla ice-cream. 'Excuse me, ma'am,' he said to Lucilla; 'we just bought this up the road a piece. Is there a freezer I could put it in?'

The pit-bull-terrier dismounted and lay on his back, allowing Mary Alice to pat his pink stomach. 'That's Lobo,' the Chicano told her; 'you his friend for life now – anybody make a fussa him, his friend for life.'

Trudi, who was either Princess's grandmother or aunt, was a rangy middle-aged woman in a floral blouse, and blue stretch slacks (ruched over her bottom so that it looked as if she was wearing a nappy beneath them). Mary Alice introduced me.

Trudi was a dignified person – she never drank straight from the bottle nor from plastic cups, she produced a crystal tumbler from her handbag.

She told me that her surname was Buford. 'I believe there is a Duke of Buford.' She had brought the guest of honour, Lucky Paradise.

Lucky Paradise was eighty-seven years old; a small trim figure, with a thin goatish face under a sweeping blond toupé. It was a face that struck me as British, a working-class face you might see in Bristol or Swansea.

Powerful spectacles gave him large goatish eyes.

He was holding a high-crowned black 4X hat and his hands were as soft and tapering and as finely manicured as a woman's. He wore a loose white shirt of coarse material, like linen, with fringes along the sleeve. The shirt dated from the 1930s, when a Hollywood cowboy, a swashbuckling pirate and Robin Hood were given essentially the same shirt by the costume designer. Around his neck was a black scarf as flat and as tight as a choker. A beaded Mexican belt hitched up a pair of baggy black trousers, that were tucked, Argentine fashion, into shiny black riding boots. The whole effect was a pastiche of the Lone Ranger, theatrical-equestrian, as if he might perform rope tricks or throw knives. Lucky was extraordinarily fit; his walk and posture were light and athletic.

I felt that his agility was dangerous because he looked so delicate – a brittle, translucent pink-and-white object, a Dresden china goat – that I was afraid he would get knocked about and chipped.

Lucky Paradise first recorded in the 1930s for Vocalion Records, for Bullet Records in the 1940s and first Mercury, then Bluebonnet Records, in the 1950s. *Oozling Mama* and *Been Using That Thing* (both Bullet releases) were his two most successful records. Today scholarly Germans collect his recordings; a Bear Family retrospective has been proposed.

Lucky was never a businessman. 'Hell, I never did read the large print, let alone the small print.' Very little money came in any more; very little ever had.

There had been an offer to play 'Stars of the Louisiana Hayride' at an air base in Manila, but he had turned it down; another to perform at a folk festival near Stuttgart, which he would have accepted but the air fare was not included, so he turned that one down too.

'I got fan letters from Ludwig van Beethoven and I gotta pay to go meet him.'

Lucky had been living in Pearland, to the south of Houston, with Mrs Kitty Laramie, a widow. From his porch he could see a Hindu temple, 'the prettiest damn thing, like a weddin' cake'.

Mrs Kitty Laramie had proposed to Lucky on 29 February but he turned her down.

Donkey George and the Bandidos were standing about with plates of food and cups of beer.

Princess called over to me. 'Joe dude! You all gotta hear this! Donkey George, you tell him about them aliens. Man, this is excellent.'

'Aw, c'mon,' muttered Donkey George bashfully. Another of the Bandidos urged him to tell the story.

'Yeah, it's a trip, man,' urged Princess.

So Donkey George told me about a summer night in 1965, when he was fifteen years old, and the bizarre events that took place near Camp Verde in the hill country. He was visiting his father, who was always drunk and had left home when Donkey George was a child.

His father lived in a dilapidated house that had been built by a family of freed slaves who had moved west after the Civil War.

'Only thing unusual about that place was the bottle tree in the front yard. Those old niggers had started it off eighty years earlier. Pulled the leaves from the upward-pointin' branches, stuck empty bottles on the ends. Some of them bottles had paint poured in 'em. That tree was like a wind-chime on a windy night. My daddy told me the niggers designed it to attract angels.'

On the night in question Donkey George had fallen asleep early. As far as he knew, his father was out in the front yard. At two in the morning the front door slammed and his father shouted, 'Stay where you are, kid.'

Donkey George could tell that his father was frightened and he thought that one of his creditors might have threatened him. He sat up and, glancing out of the window, saw, coming towards the house, not an unpaid shopkeeper but a short spectral figure that glowed in the dark.

'Way!' applauded Happy Jack, who had just come out of his grandfather's house.

The humanoid was a pearly-green colour; it had a round head, large flapping ears, and a wide slit-like mouth with no visible teeth. Donkey George reckoned it was about the size of the pit-bull-terrier, standing on his hind legs; occasionally it walked on all fours.

'No shit!' whistled Princess with delight.

'What'd you do, man?' asked one of the Bandidos. 'I would have shot the mother.'

Donkey George said that his father had been asleep in the long grass when a spaceship (like a small illuminated merry-go-round) had landed beside the creek. The humanoid Donkey George saw was just one of several. Before long he had counted five of them, all varying slightly in size, the largest being about five feet tall.

Mr Advani was listening intently. 'Those were ETs, of that you can be certain.'

For several hours the glowing beings circled the house. There was no telephone. Donkey George decided to run to a neighbour's house to notify the police. His father said he would cover his movements with a shotgun.

As soon as Donkey George stepped outside, the largest humanoid made towards him.

Immediately his father shot the humanoid; the blast knocked it over, and extinguished its inner light, and it scuttled away. Donkey George ran to the neighbour's, who could not see his father's house from their own, and were hugely sceptical, but they allowed him to use their telephone. The police accompanied Donkey George back to the ranch house.

All over the front yard there was broken glass; the bottle tree was destroyed. The humanoids had vanished, and his father was completely drunk and incoherent. The police treated the event as a false alarm.

'Ain't that bitchin'?' Princess asked me.

When Lucky unpacked his twelve-string guitar and started to play, he wore his black hat.

The songs were not country in the modern sense but cowboy folk-songs. They were not work songs, they were off-hours songs; they were to be sung by someone who had worked as a cowboy before hitting the bottle and would work as a cowboy again when he was sober.

There is a lyrical territory between 'Git Along Little Dogies' and 'Hey, Good Lookin'' – when the cowboy first frequents the honky-tonk – that Jimmie Rodgers and Floyd Tillman explored, and so did Lucky Paradise.

His voice was as dry as a road, and when he attempted to yodel it was as if an injured crow flapped across the dry road. The end of each line was met by a little wheeze.

His otherwise spare, linear guitar-playing was decorated in unexpected places by Mexican flourishes; it also emphasized the flattened sevenths that are common to both Celtic music and blues. I could hear the whole thing as a blues, or a *fado*, every line pregnant with resignation – 'Darlin', we've come to our journey's close, / This is the end of love's trail' – and the distinctive patina of many, many performances before indifferent audiences. He was no longer singing to charm fortune; instead he was singing because that was how he had used up his life – 'That's all she wrote: / Dear John, / I'll send your saddle home.'

'Listen to me, I'm real old, even older than Cockerdoody, and I'm still foolin' around, still fuckin' up.' Old goat blues about old goat age, reflections upon a goatish life, dancing goat memories:

> 'Did you ever wake up on a Sunday at dawn
> With them snakes crawlin' in your bed?
> I know you have and I have too,
> I know I would rather be dead.
> The preacher comes in to give advice,
> That is when you gotta stall . . .
> Cause if he gets to the bottle first,
> He won't leave you none at all . . .
> (*yodel ay e ay e ay e*)
> He just won't leave you none at all.'

Some were comic, mildly satirical songs; others were more placid and filled with Victorian sentiments:

> 'Remember what you promised me,
> As we set side by side,
> Beneath that ole persimmon tree,

You said you'd be my bride.
Way out in Idyho,
We're goin' to Idyho,
With a four-horse team,
We'll soon be seen
Way out in Idyho.'

The words of the songs were not the real words; Lucky was goofing, grinning, singing nursery rhymes.

What he was really singing was one long song, with a tune that kept changing ever so slightly, about the joys of distraction and idle time, and about freedom: a 'don't-fence-me-in' song, but not a landscape song, for freedom was no longer guaranteed by wide open spaces; those days were over when Lucky was a young man. Lucky was singing about freedom from work, drudgery, responsibility. The freedom to get drunk all night and the next day too, or to go fishing.

Sparling recognized this and called out. 'All right, Lucky!'

Lucky was singing a song that could be about his life; Sparling could identify a bolder and simpler version of himself in the song. It was an attractive image, even if it was granted by an 87-year-old singing goat.

If your boss is mean, quit. If your car won't run, walk. If you don't like my peaches, don't shake my tree.

The song Lucky was singing actually went: 'If you don't want to smell my smoke, Don't monkey with my gun.'

'Yes sir!' Sparling shouted. 'That's advice I would give to my own son!' He did not have a son but that was beside the point.

Everybody was clapping Lucky Paradise, whooping and passing bottles around, and calling him a good old boy. People were dancing. The braying voice was not melodious but it made people dance as a reflex, like a doctor's hammer striking the funny bone. The three black cowboys alone did not dance. Instead they stood listening to the songs attentively, clapping politely after each one, with a formal interest in the lyric but not moved to dance.

•

'Here's a little song I learned from old man Gus McAlpine; he was an old Confederate veteran. I met him on the road outa Caplen – I'd started off to a dance when I was about fifteen or sixteen years old and I had my guitar on my back. He calls over, "Lucky, let me see your guitar!" He took it and changed the tuning way on up like this – that was the old way of tuning – and he sang this here song that I'd like to sing to y'all . . .

> 'On her face was the beauty of nature,
> Her eyes they did seem to expand;
> Her hair was so rich and so brilliant,
> Tied up in a blue velvet band . . .'

I was doing the necessary arithmetic to span 130 years. The encounter would have taken place in the early 1920s. Gus McAlpine would probably have been a little younger than Lucky was now.

Mary Alice told me that she was going to cry. 'I have always loved that song; my daddy used to sing that song.' She joined in the last verse, and her singing voice was close to her talking voice.

> 'I'll be out in a year, then I'm leaving,
> But I'll still bear the name of the man
> Who spent twenty-five years in prison
> For the girl in the blue velvet band.'

Lucky was sitting on one of the sofas beside Mary Alice.

'Now, when I was a young man, I slept just about as you would expect. And, fact of the bidness, when I was singin' dance-halls I couldn't do without my sleep, or I wouldn't be good and handsome. But after, I slowed down some, been lodgin' with Miss Kittie, I just kindly forgot about sleepin', idn't that funny? I can tell you exactly all hours of the day and night when I'm up.'

'Oh baby, y'all gotta sleep some,' purred Mary Alice.

'Miss Kittie calls out, "Lucky, what the hell time do you call this?" I say, "Three twenty-five after midnight exactly, mam," say it loud and clear. So help me Hannah, I been on my toes day and night, without takin' my boots off, for months! I take my catnaps with them boots on, mam, just like a feller in the saddle would, idn't that funny?'

'Baby, you need your sleep.'

'I just stay right there in with it, and if I went out in Texas or Louisiana and said I'm eighty-seven years old, and I no longer need my sleep, and I do believe it's a miracle, you think them doctors gone want to hear that? No, mam, cause it proves medicine wrong.'

Catfish came over with a bottle of whiskey, teasing the old singer. 'Here's the damn medicine. Man, you should play some rock 'n' roll for us, move with the times.'

Sparling grabbed the bottle from Catfish. He was sitting very respectfully at Lucky's feet. 'You knew Elvis Presley, huh, Lucky? You know, so did old Mary Alice here, beside you – know him, I mean.'

Mary Alice sighed proudly. 'I do surely miss that man too.'

'Mam, when you get to eighty-seven years old, you got a powerful lot of acquaintance up yonder, and they sendin' you down the insight. Let me assure you personally that Elvis is fine and dandy.'

'Why, that's just wonderful, Lucky baby.'

'Yes, mam. I loved Elvis just like I always loved Hank Williams, another one comes to me sometimes. Elvis was a rock 'n' roller, sure enough, but I never did know of his doin' no crimes, not even chasin' after men's wives – he didn't hurt nobody. He sits with the Lord up there, givin' all Americans, regardless of creed and colour, a special greetin'.'

I wanted to know who greets the English. 'Oh, that young feller got himself shot up there in New York – what is his name? Jack Lemmon, idn't it?' It was not a question that interested Lucky.

He turned to Mary Alice again. 'Elvis is fine, I can tell

you. Just didn't look after himself, mam; went out there and got himself unfit. I myself have nearly outlived Elvis Presley twice over.'

Lucky Paradise had performed on the border radio stations in the 1930s, pirate organizations that escaped the regulations of the National Association of Broadcasters by locating themselves just south of the Rio Grande and applying for broadcasting rights from the Mexican government.

The border radio stations were equipped with extremely powerful transmitters. While most of the NAB stations broadcast with over 1,000 watts, some border transmitters would boom across North America with one million watts – they could be heard in Canada, even in Europe and Australia.

The owners of these stations tended to be mavericks. Perhaps the most notorious was 'Doctor' Brinkley, the proprietor of XERA.

Brinkley was a medical charlatan who propounded goat-gland treatment for prostate troubles; the glands of Toggenburg goats, odourless and quite compatible with those of the human being, could, he assured his thousands of listeners, rejuvenate and restore sexual drive.

The 'doctor' had no licence and only the most specious qualifications; he had made his great discovery while employed at a meat-packing plant in Kansas City. Later he developed glandular preparations that could be injected into both men and women with supposedly beneficial results.

Brinkley, who had already alarmed medical authorities in Kansas, built his station in 1931 at Villa Acuña, just across the Rio Grande from Del Rio, Texas. His hospital was set up on several floors of the Roswell Hotel in Del Rio.

XERA, like most border stations, broadcast hillbilly music (in those days the performances were generally live) and the far-reaching airwaves provided the most effective publicity a singer could hope for. XERA also featured the popular astrologers Rose Dawn (Patroness of the Sacred Order of Maya) and her mystic husband Koran. Brinkley himself was the biggest star, addressing the multitudes with his weird notions, a potent mixture of pseudo-medical theories and old-time religion.

The American Medical Association warned people that Brinkley was a dangerous quack. Brinkley, in turn, referred to his critics as the Amateur Meat-Cutters' Association and urged his listeners to trust their own instincts. They flocked to Del Rio for the miraculous treatment and in 1936 Brinkley was reportedly earning $1 million a year.

He covered himself with diamond jewellery, owned a fleet of nine Cadillacs – each emblazoned with DOCTOR BRINKLEY in rainbow letters – and built a mansion equipped with a mahogany ballroom, dancing fountains and a giant pipe organ. A private zoo contained several 300-lb Galapagos tortoises and a flock of penguins.

Over the airwaves Brinkley encouraged his listeners to settle in the Del Rio area, and the visitors and settlers he brought to the small Texas town allowed it to boom all through the Depression. The red-light district of Villa Acuña became one of the most prosperous in Mexico as the patients rushed across the border to test their restored vigour. Eventually the United States came to an agreement with the Mexican government and the fraudulent 'doctor' was put out of business. XERA was shut down.

Brinkley returned to Kansas, where, in 1941, he suffered a severe heart attack; a blood clot formed in his leg and it had to be amputated. Already bankrupt, he faced charges of mail fraud. Doctor Brinkley never went to court because he died on 26 May 1942.

I asked Lucky if he had received goat-gland treatment. 'No sir, but I do know there wadn't no harm in them boosters. Many people was the better for them – I seen that with my own eyes. I was healthy enough in them days; didn't need his help.'

Lucan and Donkey George were drinking tequila shots and Lucilla was rolling reefers.

It was getting dark and more guests kept arriving. Spike and Garland had walked over from the Horseshoe Liquor and Meat Mart. Most of the Gujeratis had arrived.

Even Miss Kinsolver came along but she kept to the side of the yard, watching people and commenting on their cleanliness. The whereabouts of the corpse concerned her. I honestly did not know if it was still in the house and the uncertainty made her even more restive.

Lucky Paradise – with some mystery, as if speaking to himself – reflected, 'Sometimes I reckon I remember bein' born, idn't that funny? Feelin' that doctor holdin' me up by my heels and spankin' me, to get me to breathin' regular. There was an old lady settin' by that bed, who was there to help out, and she called out, "Don't y'all lay another lick on that kid!"

'My daddy, Evan Paradise the Third, he'd gone bust rice-farming, and he got himself a little gasoline launch, and all them farmers had sailboats, and my daddy would tow them boats with a load of fruit and vegetables up to Houston, make a few dollars doin' that, then let them all sail on back. If there was a wind. Otherwise he would make a few dollars more, haulin' them back. We used to take an old cast net out to the bay shore and fill up a tub with shrimp, bring them on home and boil them. There was an oyster-bed back of Parr's Grove; we would catch us a basket. My mother made crab stew.

'It was my mother who loved music, ceptin' she never had the time to play it because she had thirteen kids, and I reckon I musta been the fifth or sixth. Several of them died when they was young. Two of them – Willis and Vernon – died when they was just born a day or two, and I had a brother, Samuel, die a little after I was born, gangrene from a burst gut ulcer, only eleven years old. Another sister, Rosa Clara, she off and died when she was sixteen, got bit by a mad dog and turned on into a dog herself in them fevers, howlin' and scratchin'; she dang near bit the doctor. That was when I was two or three. So I guess they called me Lucky cause I needed to be lucky.'

•

The only person missing was Ronny Sue. Mary Alice had seen her earlier in the day, near the ferry landing, and she had been in one of her rages. Happy Jack was so drunk that he had fallen asleep with his bright-pink head resting on the lowest step and his mouth wide open, his hands twitching at the wrists.

We were all listening to Lucky Paradise's stories, and the frogs and cicadas, and in the background the sea groaned impatiently like somebody trying to find a comfortable position to sleep in, or a great big dog turning round and round before settling.

The food was nearly all gone. We had eaten Donkey George's ice-cream from the beer cups.

Poor Miss Kinsolver was bothered by the mosquitoes: not so much because they were biting her but because they might be spreading Cockerdoody's illness.

The pit-bull-terrier was lazily crunching crawfish shells, and Spike and Garland were getting on very well with the Bandidos.

The Pirate's Cove contingent were talking amongst themselves; they seemed to be happy although they were wary of Princess. Whenever she went close to them, all the Gujeratis fell silent. Perhaps they felt that a pregnant girl should be indoors, away from the revelry. I think Princess recognized their disapproval: she kept shooting them very bitter glances.

Lucky went on. 'Cockerdoody and me trapped them muskrats back in the marshes. At times there were plenty, if the season was right – useda get a dollar and a half apiece for them pelts.'

Mary Alice recalled that Cockerdoody always wore a muskrat hat in cold weather.

Sparling contradicted her, insisting that it was a racoon hat.

Trudi burst out laughing. She remembered the dog that belonged to Irene, Cockerdoody's wife. 'You talkin' about dogs. Irene got herself one. It was a pure French apricot poodle; Irene called it Jezebel. Boy, every time old Cockerdoody lowered his pants that damn dog would up and bite his butt! He showed me one day. Ooh boy! It was black and blue!'

Lucky wasn't listening to Trudi and he looked up and said, 'See, I remember the time when folks left the small towns for the big cities like Houston and Dallas. And them cities jus' got bigger and bigger till people started spillin' on out the edges and these little towns took the overspill. I look about me tonight and these sure ain't the relatives of the old-timers; these ain't hardly country people at all. Most of these is new-timers. Well, heck, I ain't bearin' no grudges, so help me Hannah. I was just thinkin' how it all goes round like a danged wheel – funny, idn't it?'

I asked Lucky Paradise how often he performed.

He played when he was invited to, rather than chase engagements. 'You think that old circuit's worth a damn? It's where you gone wear yourself down. You gone see a feller that's comin' up alongside of you over there that's singin' a fine song, country song, could even be a *conjunto* song now, and you know he's gone come up on you and pass you, if you don't stay in the collar, boy. Gets too much like a damned race, playin' bookin's. Guest appearances, boy, that's where to play. You got respect for who you are.'

Suddenly there was a commotion. Ronny Sue, under cover of darkness, had crept up and thrown a powerful arm around Sparling's scrawny neck. I just saw his feet being pulled into the shadows. Everybody laughed.

'I guess that means they're reunited,' chuckled Lucilla.

Then I fell asleep on the sofa. Mary Alice woke me up an hour or so later and told me that I had been snoring. People were leaving.

It was one in the morning when we got back to the House of Blue Lights.

Mary Alice had a pint of schnapps that she had picked up from the Horseshoe Liquor and Meat Mart. She also had a video, *Pretty Woman*. We had just started to watch it when the phone rang for the first time since I'd been staying there.

I hoped it would be my friend ringing from New Orleans. I had sent her my Seven African Powers postcard (I regretted that). I would be in New Orleans in just over a week.

It wasn't a call from New Orleans, it was the Homestead begging Mary Alice to come to work because Roxie, the only night waitress, had lain on some poison ivy. Mary Alice said, 'Well, I'm still awake, I'll be on the next ferry,' and she went downstairs to start the Impala.

Nine

THE TERRIBLE EVENTS REMAIN UNCLEAR TO ME.

I woke up at seven and discovered that Mary Alice was home again, lying on her bed, sobbing.

As far as I could make out she had driven to the landing – at night the ferries are less frequent - where she had boarded the ferry and disembarked at Galveston without incident. Though tired and slightly drunk, she had handled the brakeless Impala capably.

But when Mary Alice reached the Homestead the engine had not died as it was supposed to. Instead the car crumpled into the side of the restaurant, smashing a large window and showering an elderly couple with broken glass.

The police arrived. Mary Alice was fired on the spot.

I could not understand whether Mary Alice had been arrested

for Driving When Intoxicated and released on bail put up by Captain Guidry, or (unlikely, I thought) the police had found her below the limit but (very likely) guilty of driving a vehicle without inspection stickers. The third possibility (only hinted at) was that her driving licence had been revoked for several earlier DWI charges and that she had actually been driving for some time illegally.

Mary Alice was crying so much, in such a state of shock, shaking and gibbering about being sent to Gatesville, that she was quite unable to remember what had happened. Sweet William kept licking the tears from her face.

I went to the bathroom to wash but the basin was clogged with sick.

'Baby, I'm real sorry,' Mary Alice called out in a feeble voice.

She spent all morning in bed. At lunchtime Lucilla showed up with a tray of leftovers from the wake. Mary Alice was too upset to eat.

She was beginning to make more sense and Lucilla helped her regain some perspective. Mary Alice would need a lawyer; Captain Guidry could help her with that. She would need another job. That might prove more difficult. Also she would need another car. That discounted the revoked licence possibility.

'I'm quittin' this drinkin' from here on out,' Mary Alice announced firmly, 'Joseph baby, will y'all come with me to that old AA, just the first time, to hold me to it?'

Sparling and Ronny Sue arrived, holding hands. They already seemed to be drunk but it might, of course, have been love. Both were horrified to find Mary Alice in such distress. Sparling held up a paper bag. 'We brung y'all a present. Found it down on the beach. It's kind of unusual – I figure it's got decorative potential. You ask me, it's the jawbone of a shark.'

Ronny Sue shook her head. 'Un huh! It's from a German Shepherd.'

Sparling handed Mary Alice the clean white jawbone, which

looked like a V-shaped piece of coral. Sweet William sniffed it excitedly.

'Anythin' I can do, sweetie, you just give the word,' offered Ronny Sue, gliding away backwards.

Lucilla held up a hand to stop her: she had an idea. 'Why don't we all clean this house up for her? Give old Mary Alice a fresh outlook.'

I volunteered to buy the necessary equipment (bleach, washing-up liquid, window spray) from Pirate's Cove. I picked up several boxes to put the empty bottles in as well.

All afternoon we worked, to the strains of the Rock-O-La. I cleaned the windows. Ronny Sue and Lucilla swept the floor and took the dirty clothes over to the coin-operated washing-machine at Pirate's Cove; it was meant for the motel guests but everyone used it.

All the time Mary Alice lay on her bed, clutching the jawbone and sipping Dr Pepper. Sweet William stared at us balefully. When we had finished, the House of Blue Lights looked cleaner but its inadequacies appeared more pronounced, as if the squalor had furnished the desolation. Mary Alice sat on her bed beside Sweet William. They were both blinking, daunted by their changed surroundings. Mary Alice put the jawbone on top of the television.

Outside on the deck there were now two large bags of rubbish and four boxes of bottles. I asked Sparling if there was a dump nearby. 'Dump? Heck, bubba, there's a damn swamp less than a click down the road!'

□ □

Lucan drove us to the AA meeting. It was on the island, at UTMB. We sat in the truck on the ferry; we were near the back of the boat, surrounded by raucous gulls. Lucan hated the gulls. 'They shit on my truck. Man, I'd like to shoot them.' I didn't want to tell him there was a grey blob right on the band of his hat.

•

Many of those attending the meeting (there were about fifty of us altogether) were hospitalized; a few even wore pyjamas. The majority were pale and surprised-looking, with sticking-up hair. I recognized Ross, who had sold me the bicycle.

Nearly everyone smoked. Mary Alice held my hand throughout the meeting. On my other side sat an elderly black woman wearing a floral-print trouser suit. On her head was a peaked cap, and over the badge (that would have specified a baseball team) she had taped a polaroid snapshot of herself, sitting up in a hospital bed, surrounded by colourful bouquets, with a doctor and two nurses in attendance. She told me she had recently undergone a mastectomy at UTMB – 'The Lord's given me another chance, praise be' – and the photograph was to broadcast her gratitude.

I asked the old woman how long she had been sober.

'I been sober all my life,' she replied indignantly.

So why was she at an Alcoholics Anonymous meeting?

'Why? Because it is a *spiritual* occasion, that's why.'

A short clerical man in a turquoise track suit ('I'm Murray and I'm an alcoholic') started the meeting with a preamble about the nature and intention of Alcoholics Anonymous. He asked an alcoholic called Yvonne to read the twelve steps and one called Porter to read the twelve traditions. Then somebody called Ray was called upon to 'share' – to tell the story of his drinking and how he was recovering with the support of Alcoholics Anonymous. A familiar figure came to the front of the room and sat down beside Murray. It was Willard, who had thrown up on my roof. I was fascinated.

Ray Willard's story was bleak and chaotic. He was born near El Paso and when he was five years old he realized that he was homosexual. (I hadn't gathered that about him in Austin.)

His family, whom he compared to the Kennedy clan, would never accept a sissy. So, encouraged by his father and brothers, he made a religion of sport. Ray Willard became a star athlete at high school. (That surprised me because I remembered him as fat and sweaty.)

He also became the school bully; he derived much sexual pleasure from beating up other boys, the physical closeness and submission. Around girls, Ray Willard was frightened; not of the girls themselves but that his true nature would reveal itself.

At first drink eased the terror. Very soon it was his undoing: it loosened his inhibitions and turned him into a swaggering loudmouth, eager to pick fights in parking lots. Ray usually won the fights and the girls he dated were either impressed or repulsed; either way, it prevented too much intimacy.

On the night of his high-school prom, he got howlingly drunk on Everclear and picked a fight with the captain of the swimming team. The swimming captain was drunk as well, and just as strong as Ray Willard, and a small crowd gathered to watch the fight.

Ray, who normally selected weaker opponents, realized that it was going to be a challenge. The fight lasted for much longer than he was used to and, for once, he was taking as many punches as he dealt. It was a new, strangely pleasant sensation to absorb such punishment.

Eventually Ray was knocked to the ground but he pulled the other boy down with him. The two of them rolled about on the tarmac and all the spectators could see that Ray was aroused and they started to jeer at him. Ray heard them but the Everclear and the erotic sensations were stronger than their disapproval. He rolled on top of the swimming captain and started to kiss him. He was dragged off by the disgusted spectators.

Then began Ray's darkest days. He was an outcast, rejected by his classmates and his own family. He moved to Austin to attend the University of Texas. There he tried to come to terms with his sexuality. Mostly he drank. He started to gain weight and that filled him with self-disgust.

He felt completely isolated and he dropped out of school. He found work as a window-cleaner and sometimes he served behind the counter in a liquor store. (I remembered him working in a place on West Sixth Street; that was about the time he defiled our roof.)

One day at the liquor store he received a telephone order for two cases of Wild Turkey. The woman on the telephone was called Mrs Jorgensen and she wanted to pay by credit card and have the cases delivered. Ray told her that they didn't deliver and suggested she drive to the store. Mrs Jorgensen replied that she had been banned from driving. Would he send the cases by taxi? She gave Ray her address, which was in Palma Plaza, just off West Lynn. (I knew the street well.)

Ray Willard happened to live very nearby so he offered to drop the cases off himself as soon as he got off work.

Mrs Jorgensen's large hacienda-style house was quite dark. Outside was a red Lincoln Continental. Ray knocked on the door, assuming she had gone out, but he heard a voice calling for him to enter. Inside, a back room was lit by one candle. 'Oh, I forgot to pay the electricity,' explained Mrs Jorgensen. She looked like a very old film star; her white hair was down and she was wearing a diamond tiara, diamond earrings and an amethyst necklace. Instead of a dress she was wearing a black swimsuit. 'It gets kinda hot without the AC.'

Mrs Jorgensen offered Ray a drink. They sat together in the candle-lit room and finished a whole bottle of Wild Turkey. Ray fell asleep on Mrs Jorgensen's sofa. The next morning they drank another bottle. Ray stayed at Mrs Jorgensen's house for, he thought, three days.

When Ray sobered up, he was driving the Lincoln Continental along North Lamar and in the pocket of his shirt were the title papers. The acquisition surprised him so he turned back towards West Lynn to find out if Mrs Jorgensen had really given him her car.

He pulled into Palma Plaza and saw two police cars and an ambulance. Ray started to panic. The police noticed the car and stopped him. Mrs Jorgensen had been stabbed to death. Ray thought he was going to be sick. The police had already arrested the murderer, a teenager called Norris Garcia. (The name sparked a memory of the murder although I hadn't been aware that it was so close to where we lived.)

The whereabouts of Mrs Jorgensen's car had been puzzling them. Ray was taken to the police station on Fifth Street for questioning.

He couldn't remember a thing and that terrified him. Eventually, he was released. The murder had taken place some twelve hours after he had been seen driving away from the house and he was not implicated.

The strange experience shook him and he decided to stop drinking. He went to a treatment centre, then attended AA regularly. He had now been sober for six years.

Through AA in Austin he met Clyde, who became his lover. Clyde and Ray opened a stationery shop near Rice University in Houston in 1989. Early in 1993 an armed robber shot Clyde in the side of the face. Now Clyde was out of hospital and seeing a specialist in Galveston who was going to reconstruct his shattered jaw.

That explained why I had seen Ray Willard outside the Maxillo-Facial Surgery.

The violence of the story and the continual presence of physical pain struck me. The alcoholic aspect was almost secondary.

When Ray had finished, others chimed in – some to congratulate him on his progress, some to identify their own stories with his; others just wanted to talk.

Nobody had looked beyond the alcohol. It was as if they were all listening to a foreign language, only a few words of which they recognized.

One old man stood up and squared his shoulders like a boxer. Punching the air, he warned, 'Ray, I was at Pearl Harbor. You gotta be on guard, son. Step Thirteen will take you back there.' That sounded frighteningly cryptic.

There were so many tears shed, by both men and women, that I was reminded of *The Oprah Winfrey Show*. The meeting ended with a recital of the Lord's Prayer. The prayer sounded highly insincere.

I wondered about drunken Jews and Muslims and I questioned Murray.

'It's real interdenominational. Who says it's to Jesus Christ, man? It's to the Higher Power.'

I asked Murray if he felt at all priestly when he conducted the meeting.

'All I feel is that I am an alcoholic, man.'

Lucan was waiting outside the hospital to drive us back to the peninsula. He said he had been watching a fire on the beach. 'Some old wrecked car belongin' to a nigger – went up like dynamite.'

'Was it a Volkswagen Rabbit?'

Lucan scratched his neck at the back of his hat. 'Time I got there, I couldn't tell what it was. Somethin' 'bout that size, sure.'

He had also solved Mary Alice's transport problems; she could drive Cockerdoody's Plymouth.

□ □

Lucilla was at the House of Blue Lights; she wanted to know how Mary Alice had got on. Mary Alice told the story of Ray Willard and burst into tears.

Lucilla put her arms around her. 'Oh honey, you're just drained. You're just exhausted, honey,' she muttered soothingly. Lucilla suggested that we all go over to her trailer for some chicken gumbo. Lucan shouted, 'Lucilla's famous chicken gumbo! Hot damn, Mary Alice!'

Lucilla's trailer was mostly a kitchen. She had a catering-size deep-fryer and a huge coin-operated spin-drier. The curtains, the cloth that covered the sofa, the cushions on the picnic chairs and the bedspread were all tie-dyed.

We watched a videotape of the Country Music Awards; there was a lot of choreographed dancing, which surprised me because it was an informal show otherwise. When it was over we took the picnic chairs outside onto the scrubby verge. Mary Alice wasn't hungry.

Lucilla filled three cereal bowls with a steaming dark-green jelly that she ladled out of a ceramic slow-cooker. She opened a packet of saltine crackers and offered us drinks. Lucan chose beer. Considering Mary Alice, I chose tea. Lucilla told me she had some special tea that she wanted to finish but she might have put too much honey in it.

She produced a large kilner jar of some cloudy sepia liquid, filled two beakers with ice, and poured us both a draught of the brew, which did not taste like tea at all. I thought of it as honey water.

The chicken gumbo was a swampy concoction; the main ingredients, okra and herbs, were the vegetation in a salty and gelatinous pond where tiny yellow chillies swam around like angry goldfish and hunks of deathly-white chicken (with goosepimple skin) and even hen's feet floated just beneath the surface. Everything seemed to be slithering about.

Lucan was wolfing it down, exclaiming that it was a true Port Arthur chicken gumbo. To me it looked forbidding, food from the Black Lagoon. Lucilla asked me, 'You think you could handle more tea?'

She brought out some Rocky Road ice-cream and her tin tray of loose marijuana.

Mary Alice asked her to play 'that soulful tape, you know, Betty Lavette'.

We were sitting under the gleaming stars and the sea was making a lot of noise, moaning.

The tea was extraordinary; its taste grew more and more intense. It was like wild honey or honey produced by big fat bees.

'What kind of tea is this, Lucilla?'

'Bolivar tea.'

Lucilla placed the stereo speakers in the window of the trailer, pointing outwards. The music Mary Alice had chosen was Southern Soul, the kind that is virtually Secular Gospel.

All the singers were women and all the songs were ballads. Betty Lavette pleaded 'Let Me Down Easy'. Doris Allen protested that she had been left 'A Shell Of A Woman'. Peggy Scott practically wept – 'Every Little Bit Hurts'. Each singer sounded sadder and mightier than the last, for it was proud melancholy, expressed by noble women.

I closed my eyes and imagined I was listening to a woman on the desolate shore. She was singing (as lonely country people, black and white, are supposed to sing to trains) to the mournful sea and the restless rhythm of the waves. I thought it might be the ghost of Kiamatia, describing a vision in a plaintive and attenuated hymn; then I thought it could be Mary Alice with her singing voice that is close to her talking voice. Her song would sound thinner than the songs on the tape but the words and the duende would be as clearly expressed.

Lucan drove us back to the house. Something in the marsh made a resounding splash as we climbed the stairs. Mary Alice smiled. 'It's that old 'gator.'

Lucan bristled like a hound. He leapt silently down the steps, back to the truck. He pulled a deer rifle from behind the seat and loaded. Two shots skimmed low across the water.

There were screams from Miss Kinsolver's trailer and, nearer to us, the alarmed flapping of heavy wings.

'What was that?' I asked Mary Alice.

'Oh, an alligator with wings,' she said with a laugh.

□ □

The next morning I went to Galveston and bought a bus ticket for New Orleans. I would leave at the weekend. I wasn't quite sure where I would sleep when I got there and I had come to the conclusion that my accommodation could only be arranged if I was actually there to arrange it.

Near the bus depot there was a Western Fried Chicken stand. Outside it, in the forecourt, hovered Henry Glover. He had cut his jeans from the knees down into ribbons, to make denim shorts with an extended fringe. His legs were a purplish colour, darker than the complexion of his face.

He pulled a cigarette-end from his pocket and lit it with a match from a book. 'You have to come down from the mountain for your food. The weather's no good, foggy. They got all kinds, English people and shit. Some beautiful houses provided – little ones with sloped floors. The International Art World. First condition: Poor people get in for nothin'.'

'Was your car burnt?'

'It does not exist. Except as a memory of the memory.'

'Were you hurt?'

He had not been there at the time of the fire; he had been contemplating an instructive piece of driftwood further down the beach.

'What about the pictures?'

'Same, sure.' Henry Glover was stoic. I asked if he knew who had done it.

'I gotta idea, oh yes. That English kid.' I thought he was blaming me for a moment. 'Reads the funny papers and tells you the jokes.' He meant Monty Richardson. 'There is a club. They goes out botherin' people. They collectin' grants for this behaviour. That English kid wants to go places: he tell them there a urban Afro-American sleepin' in a car down there. He becomes majestic; if they have a majestic sense, it is out of sight.' He was quite angry, raving for a while about kings and emperors.

'Where will you go?' I asked him.

'That is the decision I am this very moment encircling.'

'Can you afford a bus ticket?'

'Difficulties, related principally to financial enquiries.'

'Where are you considering?'

'Libya.'

'I've just bought a ticket for New Orleans.' I was trying to imply that we were both moving on.

'N'Awlins, how you pronounce it. I'd go for the Bucket of Blood.' This statement made him smile, flickeringly, as at a happy memory.

'What's the Bucket of Blood?' I thought it was a football game.

'Wild Squatoolas, Red Frontier Hunters.'

'What sport?'

'Tribal domination, baby. These are people with the characterization of endangered birds – you know, long waving feathers. They can only be glimpsed.'

'Have you got enough money?'

□ □

I asked Mary Alice if she thought Monty Richardson could have burnt Henry Glover's car.

She was not very concerned. 'I guess he might could have. Y'all understand, these kids *do* go for bums. Nobody wants bums all here. Many of them are kinda derailed and that's real bad for tourism.'

I was horrified. 'They may as well start lynching people.'

'No, honey. They draw the line.'

Staying at the House of Blue Lights had become arduous. Mary Alice had run out of money and Captain Guidry had gone back to his wife in Houma, Louisiana.

Sobering up was taking a great emotional toll on her. She spent a lot of time crying. I felt that Mary Alice was getting more fragile by the day.

The house grew untidy again; that was a welcome transformation.

I suggested that she would be better attempting to stop drinking when she was in a more stable situation. I urged her to find another job as soon as possible.

Princess went into labour and Mr Advani drove her over to UTMB.

I asked Lucilla why he had taken her and she told me that the father was Mr Advani's nephew, Manmohan. Princess hadn't known that Manmohan was already married to a Gujerati girl. When Manmohan urged Princess to have an abortion, Sparling had threatened to shoot him. Manmohan, terrified, had fled to Vancouver.

To keep the peace, Mr Advani had offered to help Princess support the child.

Sparling had complicated the situation by proposing to marry Princess.

'What about Ronny Sue?'

'Well, they ain't married.'

The arrangement was that Sparling would be the baby's father but remain otherwise involved with Ronny Sue.

Princess had teased Sparling for a while by accepting and rejecting his proposal.

Sparling had an idea that the baby might look like him. 'Heck, we've both got Indian blood.'

Princess would prefer to control the mystery of the baby's provenance herself. I guessed that she would claim Karim, the frozen-yoghurt vendor, as the father.

Lucilla had only told me about Manmohan because I was leaving.

After four days of sobriety, Mary Alice relapsed on a bottle of Wild Irish Rose that Ronny Sue left at the House of Blue Lights. In her intoxication she was revitalized; she told me that she was a born survivor, that she had been through worse times.

She was going to ask Lucan if she could dance at his clubs in Sulphur. In the meantime there were establishments on the island.

'But, Mary Alice,' I suggested, as tactfully as possible, 'aren't your dancing days over now?'

'Joseph honey, ain't you heard of comebacks? Ain't y'all seen Joan Collins?'

'Joan Collins isn't dancing in topless bars.'

'Oh, hush. I got dimples. Cheekbones. Eyelashes. Baby, that's just where I'm startin' from.'

On Saturday morning she drove me to the Galveston bus depot in Cockerdoody's Plymouth. Mary Alice complained the steering column was out of sync. Whenever she turned a corner she had to heave the wheel around, sighing, 'Hoo diggy!'

Sweet William licked my arm for ten minutes.

Before she kissed me goodbye, Mary Alice squeezed my hand. 'Now, Joseph, anythin' goes wrong, you just head on back here, y'all know that.' Then she drove away, swerving a little because of the steering column.

I carried my case into the waiting-room and I felt that all my life

I had been distancing myself from people. I thought of Mary Alice swerving along, a kind woman taking in strangers.

There was a familiar smell of cigarettes and seaweed. From behind the door, a reedy voice sang out:

'Two way puck away!
Two way puck away!'

Books, Libraries & Bookshops

It should be obvious that my intention in writing this book was not to produce an academic document but to give a necessarily subjective account of my time by the Gulf of Mexico and to retell the stories – verifiable or otherwise – that caught my fancy. If I am, deliberately in this case, more of a magpie than a historian, I have gleaned bright pieces of information from a number of written sources. Here are the richest of them:

Johnnie Allan – *Memories*.
Roy Bedichek – *Karankaway Country*.
Anne Brindley – *Jane Long* (Southwestern Historical Quarterly, vol. 46, October 1952).
John Broven – *South to Louisiana*.

Gary Cartwright – *One Last Shot* (Texas Monthly, June 1993).
Jonathan Cott – *Wandering Ghost.*
Cyclone Covey (trans.) – *Cabeza de Vaca's Adventures in the Unknown Interior of America.*
A. Pat Daniels – *Bolivar! Gulf Coast Peninsula.*
James M. Day – *The Karankawas.*
Philip Durham & Everett L. Jones – *The Adventures of the Negro Cowboys.*
Gene Fowler & Bill Crawford – *Border Radio.*
Mary Gehman – *The Howard Johnson's Shootout: A Retrospective* (Dialogue, vol. 95, January/February 1993).
Peter Guralnick – *Feel Like Going Home.*
Lost Highway.
Sweet Soul Music.
Searching for Robert Johnson.
David G. McComb – *Galveston, A History.*
Bill C. Malone – *Country Music USA.*
Ray Miller – *Ray Miller's Galveston.*
Nahziryah Monastic Community, Nazir Order of the Purple Veil – *The Book of the Order.*
W. Newcomb – *The Indians of Texas.*
Patrick M. Reynolds – *Texas Lore.*
Lyle Saxon, Edward Dreyer & Robert Tallant – *Gumbo Ya Ya.*
Ron Stone – *Disaster at Texas City.*
Robert Tallant – *Voodoo in New Orleans.*
Melanie Wiggins – *They Made Their Own Law.*
Charles Reagan Wilson & William Ferris – *Encyclopaedia of Southern Culture.*

I must also acknowledge the helpfulness and efficiency of the staff at the Rosenberg Library in Galveston, at the libraries of the University of Texas at Austin, and of the curators of the Louisiana Collection at Tulane University in New Orleans; as well as the assistance given at countless bookshops across Texas and Louisiana.

In England, in addition to the British Library, I found the American Museum in Bath very useful. Also in Bath I am especially grateful to the Chandor family at Bankes Books and to all the staff at Waterstone's.